Praise for *The End of Our Exploring*

Doubt has become very popular in the last few years. Many times though, doubt never takes the doubter anywhere for answers. Matt shows us how to question well and actually let our doubts take us to God.

DARRIN PATRICK, lead pastor of The Journey St. Louis, author of *For the City* and *Church Planter*

I wish I had read this book a long time ago! Learning to question well is one of the most important things we can teach young people to do. I will be recommending this book to the many young people I work with every day.

SEAN MCDOWELL, educator, speaker, author of *Apologetics for a New Generation*

Finally a book that encourages us to doubt our doubts! Well, not exactly, but Anderson does a good job of discerning the various types of questions and doubt we experience. The goal is not to celebrate doubt but to help us learn to ask the questions that lead to an increasingly mature and dynamic faith.

MARK GALLI, editor of *Christianity Today*

Never mind the hand-wringing about "young evangelicals." Read Matthew Lee Anderson and you'll feel much better.

JOHN WILSON, editor of *Books & Culture*

This is a personal, extended meditation on the question, which is to say that it does not try to be hip or current in any way whatsoever. This very quality, its calm, patient perusing, yields the gifts that the book will give to the reader who pushes through the first question ("why should I read *this*?") and simply decides to go exploring with Matt.

TYLER WIGG-STEVENSON, author, *The World Is Not Ours to Save* and *Brand Jesus*

Christians are often accused of being unwilling to ask the hard questions. Matthew Anderson not only ⟨...⟩ core to the Christian life, but equip ⟨...⟩ ef- fectively engage in this practic ⟨...⟩ think, understand, and live for the go⟨...⟩

PAUL SPEARS, director of Torr⟨...⟩

D1510951

In a world where "dialogue" and "conversation" are buzzwords but rarely well practiced, and where doubt and questioning seem to be more about a scene than a search for truth, Matthew Lee Anderson's *The End of Our Exploring* comes as a breath of fresh air. Clearheaded, personal, witty, and wise, Anderson's book presents a sensible framework for epistemology that is sorely needed today.

BRETT MCCRACKEN, author of *Hipster Christianity: When Church & Cool Collide* and *Gray Matters: Navigating the Space between Legalism & Liberty*

Over the years, I've realized that my wisest, most interesting, most enjoyable friends share at least one common trait: they all ask good questions. They're curious, openhearted, aware of all the vistas they haven't yet explored, seeking out truth, goodness, and beauty in places they haven't yet discovered. Matthew Lee Anderson's new book explains why I find this trait so attractive in my friends (hint: it's the virtue of *hope*), and he explains how I can cultivate that quality for myself while avoiding its pitfalls. After closing his book, I'm better equipped to heed Jesus' simple command, "Ask."

WESLEY HILL, author of *Washed and Waiting: Reflections on Christian Faithfulness and Homosexuality*

In *The End of Our Exploring*, Matt Lee Anderson recovers a lost art—that of questioning well. If you have questions about faith, life, or pain, then this book will equip you to ask questions to challenge and guide you. He describes how questioning can be a pathway to beauty, love, and redemption. Relevant and engaging, Anderson's work has personally changed the way I ask questions.

PETER GREER, president and CEO of HOPE International, author of *The Spiritual Danger of Doing Good*

For years, Matt has challenged me to ask the right questions. This practice has deepened my love for God and the gospel and greatly helped me approach the countless nuances of both ministry and personal life. He has eloquently captured the essence of this helpful practice in *The End of Our Exploring*. As usual, Matt is brilliantly engaging and humbly transparent as he illuminates the importance of thoughtful exploration and the dangers of asking the wrong questions. I highly recommend everyone reads this book.

STEPHEN MILLER, worship leader, author of *Worship Leaders, We Are Not Rock Stars*

A thought-provoking, question-stirring book that opens the windows of the mind and allows fresh air to blow through our debates and discourse. You may never look at a question the same way again.

TREVIN WAX, managing editor of The Gospel Project, author of *Clear Winter Nights, Gospel Centered Teaching,* and *Counterfeit Gospels*

Matt Anderson has questions. But he also has answers. But he also has questions about those answers, and answers about where our questions come from, where they take us, what they reveal and conceal, how they work, what kind of people we questioners are, and what our questioning is for. Open your mind for this book the way you would open your hands for a gift, so you can grab onto something solid at last.

FRED SANDERS, associate professor of theology, Torrey Honors Institute, Biola University

Matt Anderson excels at asking good questions. In this book, he thanks several people who he says are responsible for teaching him to question well. I'm glad they did. Matt understands and describes in this book how faith can be big enough for doubt, and how questions are better than answers sometimes. Even more important, Matt understands—unlike many in his generation—that the goal of questioning is truth, or more accurately the God who is Truth and is big enough for our questions.

JOHN STONESTREET, speaker and author for Breakpoint and Summit Ministries

Matthew Lee Anderson challenges us to examine the heart behind our inquiries and embrace the God-glorifying design of asking questions—to see them as opportunities to edify and encourage, to grow in our faith. *The End of Our Exploring* is a wonderful gift to readers of all stripes; I can't recommend it highly enough.

AARON ARMSTRONG, author of *Contend* and *Awaiting a Savior*; blogger, bloggingtheologically.com

Anderson's style exhibits a tenderness for his subject and his reader that can only have come from the constant practice of his book's ideals. He isn't shouting, "Question! Discuss!" like many contemporary reformers do. Rather, he invites the church to ask questions using a tone that fits with question-asking—that is, he invites us with patience, love, good faith, and wonder.

PETER DAVID GROSS, executive director of Wheatstone Ministries, editor of *The Examined Life*

The End of Our Exploring is a book questioning our questions, taking us through our doubts and struggles to a richer faith. Matthew Lee Anderson brings his needed perspective into the idea that we can and should question well. For those wondering where their questions fit in a life of faith *The End of Our Exploring* is a can't-miss book.

TYLER BRAUN, author of *Why Holiness Matters: We've Lost Our Way—But We Can Find It Again*

Matt Anderson is asking all the right questions about questioning. But this book is neither a detached academic exploration of various forms of questioning nor an angsty defense of the glories of doubt. Instead, Anderson begins rightly with the questions God asks of us and then proceeds to offer us a clear and compelling vision of how to question well over a lifetime. My only question is, Why did someone not write something this important sooner?

JOHN DYER, executive director of Communications and Educational Technology, Dallas Theological Seminary, author, *From the Garden to the City: The Redeeming and Corrupting Power of Technology*

The End of Our Exploring by Matthew Lee Anderson is smart, challenging, and personal. This book will change the way you question, which is to say it will change the way you think about life, faith, and everything in between.

SCOTT MCCLELLAN, author of *Tell Me a Story*

With delightful and at times lyrical prose, Anderson argues that faith is not opposed to asking hard questions about life and reality, but in fact that good inquiry strengthens faith and leads to a deeper trust in God. And the more we understand and trust God, the more meaningful life becomes. By providing a theology and roadmap to questioning, Anderson has done the church and the academy a huge favor.

JIM BELCHER, author of *In Search of Deep Faith: A Pilgrimage into the Beauty, Goodness and Heart of Christianity*

Matthew Lee Anderson is one of the brightest people I know, and when he speaks, I listen. In *The End of Our Exploring*, he tackles our deepest faith questions and doubts head-on. Read it and you'll doubtlessly be challenged.

JONATHAN MERRITT, author of *A Faith of Our Own: Following Jesus Beyond the Culture Wars*

Matthew Lee Anderson

The End of
Our Exploring

A Book About Questioning and
the Confidence of Faith

MOODY PUBLISHERS
CHICAGO

Scripture quotations marked ESV are taken from *The Holy Bible,
English Standard Version*. Copyright © 2000, 2001 by Crossway Bibles, a division of
Good News Publishers. Used by permission. All rights reserved.
Scripture quotations marked NKJV are taken from the *New King James Version*. Copyright
© 1982 by Thomas Nelson, Inc. Used by permission. All rights reserved.
Scripture quotations marked NASB are taken from the *New American Standard Bible*, Copyright © 1960, 1962, 1963, 1968, 1971, 1972, 1973, 1975, 1977, 1995 by The Lockman
Foundation. Used by permission. (www.Lockman.org)
Scripture quotations marked NIV are taken from the Holy Bible, New International Version, NIV. Copyright © 1973, 1978, 1984, 2011 by Biblica, Inc.™ Used by permission
of Zondervan. All rights reserved worldwide. www.zondervan.com. The "NIV" and
"New International Version" are trademarks registered in the United States Patent and
Trademark Office by Biblica, Inc.™
Scripture quotations marked KJV are taken from the King James Version.

Published in association with the literary agency of
Wolgemuth and Associates, Inc.

Edited by Brandon O'Brien
Cover design: DogEared Design
Cover image: iStock #293859
Interior design: Smartt Guys design

ISBN: 978-0-8024-0652-1

We hope you enjoy this book from Moody Publishers. Our goal is to provide high-quality, thought-provoking books and products that connect truth to your real needs and
challenges. For more information on other books and products written and produced
from a biblical perspective, go to www.moodypublishers.com or write to:

Moody Publishers
820 N. LaSalle Boulevard
Chicago, IL 60610

1 3 5 7 9 10 8 6 4 2

Printed in the United States of America

To the faculty of the Torrey Honors Institute
and especially its founder, John Mark Reynolds.
Without them, this book would not exist.

Contents

A Beginning

━━━━━━━━ ❦ ━━━━━━━━

> Old men ought to be explorers
> Here and there does not matter
> We must be still and still moving
> Into another intensity
> For a further union, a deeper communion.
>
> —T. S. ELIOT[1]

This book explores what it means to ask a question and treats questioning as a kind of exploration. It is a book that poses a series of questions and—while acknowledging every ounce of the irony—proposes what might be considered answers. What moves us to ask a question? Are there questions we should be impelled to ask? Are there questions we should avoid? What sort of answer would it take to move us to give up our questions? These are the lines of thought this book opens, the paths through an unknown world that I attempt to clear away.

Others have ably defended the place of questioning within the Christian life.[2] My pursuit is related but heads off in a slightly

---

1. T. S. Eliot, *Four Quartets* (New York: Harcourt Brace Jovanovich, 1971), 34.
2. Most prominently, see: David Dark, *The Sacredness of Questioning Everything* (Grand Rapids: Zondervan, 2009). Also: Rachel Held Evans, *Evolving in Monkey Town: How a Girl Who Knew All the Answers Learned to Ask the Questions* (Grand Rapids: Zondervan, 2010).

different direction. I am chiefly concerned to explore whether we can question *well* and what such questioning might look like. The inquiry tosses us into the middle of things. It is an evaluative question, one that challenges us who have taken up the method without considering where it might take us. "Where have you come from and where are you going?" is the question the angel of the Lord poses to Hagar as she flees Sarai. Where do we inquire from and where will our pursuit take us? And will our exploring lead us home, even if we arrive with a limp?

The snub-nosed philosopher Socrates famously suggested that the "unexamined life is not worth living."[3] We remember little about him except that bit, and that his insistent pestering eventually got him killed. His general point goes too far, in my opinion. Those with severe mental disabilities have lives worth living, even if they may not be able to examine them as others might. But I borrow from Socrates' dictum to introduce one of my own: *The unexamined question is not worth asking.* It has the same element of hyperbole and so all the same problems. But it also neatly lays out the hypothesis that we will pursue.

My intent, then, is to question our questions—and with them our questioning. The two concepts—questions and questioning—are closely related but not precisely identical. If a person asks a question, it does not mean they have begun "questioning" or "exploring" or "inquiring." If someone asks us when the Cubs last won the World Series, we can have a good laugh and then deliver the bad news: back when Teddy Roosevelt was president, or before any of us were alive. They have successfully asked a question. But unless they have some interest in the answer, some fundamental concern about the result, then we would hardly say they have begun "questioning." Those who question (rather than merely *ask questions*) have something wrapped up in their pursuit, such that

---

3. Plato, *Apology*. Available through Project Gutenberg, trans. by Benjamin Jowett.

the meaning of their lives will be altered depending on what they see (or fail to see).

Questioning is a form of life, a habit, and even a disposition. It is one way our loves and desires take shape—and a practice that also shapes our desires. There is a peculiar quality that the questioning person cultivates, an openness to the world before them and a willingness to consider events with the hope that they might learn something. Their inquiries don't stay on the surface, either of the world or their own soul. They explore the *why* and the *how* to discern the fundamental shape of things. Their openness goes beyond the possibility they are wrong toward the active reconsideration of their stances when given reasons that compel them to do so.

Questioning makes itself known through the form of our inquiries, just as anger makes itself known to us when we get angry and we recognize courage when people act courageously. The questions we pose in conversation, in prayer, and to ourselves are like the vital signs a doctor checks. Those that flow from a questioning life sound and feel different from those that do not. It is partly the burden of this book to explore such a life in a way that we can begin to detect the difference.

My path over the terrain, though, is not necessarily a straightforward one. In my opening chapter, I introduce a variety of loosely connected themes that I return to in various ways throughout the book. It is something of an initial stroll around the grounds to note the main features, while subsequent chapters will fill in the details. Chapter 2 takes up the question of whether questions are neutral. And in the third chapter I consider the peculiar relationship of doubt and questioning, which are similar and related postures but not identical. Conflating them has been the source of a great deal of confusion.

Given that it makes little sense to think about questioning without considering what might count as an "answer," that is my pursuit in the fourth chapter. In chapter 5, I attempt to give an account of how our inquiries relate to the world around us and how our questions take their shape.

From there, I'm off in a different direction: I explore what it means for our questioning to be liberated from the various threats and obstacles to it (chapter 6) and try to explain what role questioning might play in our churches (chapter 7). In chapter 8 I attempt to show what good questioning and inquiry means within friendships, and what good friendship looks like with people that we don't agree with. Chapter 9 is more practical in nature, and the final chapter is more of a postscript meant to bring things together. Beyond that, I have included two appendices of essays I originally wrote for *Boundless* that may be of interest to those who are or know students at Christian colleges and those who have left the faith. A confession of my gratitude finishes the work and can be read even if the appendices are not.

How then shall we begin? We are, of course, already underway. We have made our start, our first step, which in a world bound by stasis is the hardest and most uncertain. The step out the door begins the adventure, which is why so many of us tend to stay home.

I

A Few Initial Thoughts about
the Questioning Life

With what end in view do you again and again walk along difficult and laborious paths? —AUGUSTINE[1]

I have never really doubted whether God exists. That may be the wrong sort of thing to admit at the opening of a book about questioning, but it's true. I have considered the arguments on each side and have done so with as much honesty as I can drum up. But those inquiries were mostly prompted by people around me—friends and family who stood at the water's edge of unbelief wondering whether they should attempt a swim. I looked along with them but found the prospect wanting. To me, that order and rationality are essential to the universe, rather than accidental, remains the most persuasive explanation.

But I have doubted whether God is good, and whether He will be good to me. The uncertainty has pressed on me, bending both soul and body beneath its weight. I have felt the terrors of

1. Augustine et al., *The Confessions of St. Augustine* (New York: P. F. Collier & Son, 1909), 4.12.18.

His judgment and the horrors of His indifference. These moments were often accompanied by confrontations with my own sin, but other times they arose out of my frustrated sense of entitlement, which I experienced as rejection. These moments were "intellectual," but went deeper even than what we normally call "emotions." I felt as though my life depended upon finding satisfaction and that my bones would rot if there was no relief. "I would have despaired," the psalmist writes, "unless I had believed I would see the goodness of the Lord in the land of the living."[2] When we consider the possibility that God will not be good to us, we stand on the precipice of despair and peer into the darkness below. To do so with a cool detachment that comes from treating the question as "merely academic" is to miss the point. To answer wrongly or not to be answered at all—on this nothing less than the universe depends.

Our anxieties sometimes shift, though. These days, I am more doubtful of seeing my own goodness in the land of the living than I am of seeing God's. He has already proven Himself in the death and resurrection of Jesus. It is I who am in question. "What must I do to inherit eternal life?" is the inquiry the ruler poses to Jesus.[3] The question signals a profound uncertainty, a sense that we are responsible for our lives and their destinations. The moment we pose it, we move down a path of confronting our own incapacity to attain salvation, a path that takes us to the limits of our own holiness and places us in need of God's. The question itself reminds us that it is we who are under judgment, not God, and that all we do is only enough to place us in need of grace.

I mention these questions only because I have asked them at various points in my life and because we start from what we

---

2. Psalm 27:13 (NASB).

3. Luke 18:18 (ESV).

know. But not everyone's uncertainties have unsettled them to the degree that mine sometimes have. And it is quite possible that Socrates was wrong and maybe no one's should. The writer of Ecclesiastes, a friend to inquirers everywhere, knew that "in much wisdom is much vexation, and he who increases knowledge increases sorrow."[4] Questions that grip us are rarely comfortable, which makes a life pursuing them seem strange to a people preoccupied with comfort and security. It's not easy to sell a tradition whose main representatives, like Solomon and Socrates, faced depression or involuntary death.[5]

Instead, we often hurry through disruptions as though nothing of fundamental importance is at stake. When goodness is called into question, when we are confronted by a dilemma and can see no way through, when a choice between the comfort of silence and gently rebuking a friend lies before us—these are the moments when we are most tempted to retreat and avoid the pressing burden of the unknown. We are rarely in danger of examining to excess, especially when the subject is the shape of our own lives. The sports page and celebrity magazine captivate us and with a good deal less discomfort. Our tendency is to avoid, to inoculate ourselves against unsettling questions with an endless titillation of trivialities. It is better not to be disturbed or to disturb.

Even so, we cannot escape when the questions come upon us. Most of us don't start questioning by hunting for subjects to explore. We feel our questions the deepest when they come over us, slowly pressing upon us until they can no longer be ignored. The mother whose child insistently asks "Why?" may herself catch the habit. The man whose friend's marriage falls apart might be moved to consider his own. The student unable to respond to

---

4. Ecclesiastes 1:18 (ESV).

5. Was Solomon depressed? Probably not. But Ecclesiastes, which is at least written in a Solomonic way, isn't exactly a chipper book.

an argument may find herself stifling a nagging disquiet that all may not be well. Sometimes questions *perturb* us, which is a lovely and forgotten word: they fill us with an unsettled awareness that, despite their stable appearance, our lives are yet open before us.

THE ANATOMY OF QUESTIONING

What happens when we question? The practice is one of our most common ways of interacting with the world, yet its mechanics remain ambiguous. And despite a few millennia of asking questions, few philosophers have examined questioning directly.[6]

When we assert something, we make a claim that may be true or false. We say that it is sunny outside with all the declarative confidence of people who have looked outside our window and seen the orb hanging in the blue. It's a trivial example, sure, and the more complicated the world gets, the more challenging such assertions become. But the grammar of the sentence, the *indicative mood*, is how we describe the world with the concepts we've inherited.

A question has a different nature, though, and constitutes a different relationship between us and the world before us. It points us toward the unknown rather than the known, drawing our attention toward some feature that is currently hidden to us. Behind the English "question" lies the Latin *quaestio*, which also connotes *seeking out*. In that sense, questions send our attention away from ourselves toward something else. They take us out on an adventure, even when we question ourselves. For by asking, "What is the character of my soul?" we must momentarily stand apart from ourselves in order to find out the answer.

Questioning is a form of our desire. Even while our inquiries often take an intellectual form, they come from wellsprings deeper

---

6. See *The Philosophy of Curiosity* by Ilhan Inan for a good example of someone who gives it a sporting try. Ilhan Inan, *The Philosophy of Curiosity* (New York: Routledge, 2012).

than the mind. We do not always choose our questions, any more than we choose our spouses. Our questions drag us about like chariots, which is precisely why letting them go can be so hard. They make us feel as though there is *something* incomplete that we desire to resolve. Our desire for satisfaction may be stronger or weaker, may intensify or wane, but it is always present.

We should think through this *something* that we feel is missing. Those who work with art sometimes speak of "negative space," or the area where something *isn't*. Consider the FedEx logo: the name of the company is spelled out in solid colors, which the eye detects instantly. But the space between the "E" and the "x" makes an arrow, to remind us of their purpose as a shipping company. Or rather, the "E" and the "x" leave an arrow out, imply an arrow that *isn't* there. It's hard to know which way to put it. For a long time, I never noticed it. After someone pointed it out, it became the only thing I could see.

But negative space isn't everywhere. Nor can we make negative space out of thin air, so to speak. I couldn't point to an empty glass cage and say it's where a lion *isn't*. It would remain an empty space, even if I attached an "artist's statement" to the contrary. Negative space takes its shape from the objects that surround it. We can only discern the missing arrow in the FedEx logo because the "E" and the "x" are present.

In a similar way, questioning draws our attention to the negative spaces of the world. We consistently encounter facts and experiences that we have to incorporate into our understanding for them to be meaningful. But what we encounter sometimes stretches our frameworks to the point of breaking them. This is particularly true when tragedy strikes. Our moral and political categories offered no meaningful explanation for the tragedy of 9/11. "How could this happen?" "What shall we call it?" "Who could do such a thing?" These and other questions forced themselves upon us and have only lost their force through the reassuring illusion of our security—and our own forgetfulness. But in those first days, we were confronted by a host of unknowns. The fragments of our knowledge about Al Qaeda, about our own security, about a suddenly unstable world left more negative spaces than they filled.

But we can only recognize gaps in our knowledge because we already know something. We ask if it is sunny outside because we know there is a sun, that it comes up, that we are inside and that there is an outside. All these claims are interconnected, and we may affirm them with different degrees of confidence. But they combine to shape the unknown about whether it will be cloudy or not today.[7] They create a space that our inquiry attempts to fill. In the case of 9/11, our understanding of America's invulnerable security proved to have a massive hole, leaving us grasping to discern how and why the airplanes had been hijacked.

Consider one of the early responses to Jesus and His ministry. After He heals a blind and mute man in Matthew 12, the gaping crowd asks, "Can this be the Son of David?"[8] The question is an important one, but so is what it presumes: the people already think they know (from the Old Testament) what it means to be the son of David. And they have their experience of Jesus and His power. What they don't have, the *something* that drives their wonder, is clarity about whether Jesus is the one who fits their expectations. They're exploring what's unknown to them, the negative space between the concept of the Messiah and the person of Jesus.[9]

We associate questioning with youthfulness and for under-

---

7. Unless one happens to live in Phoenix, where it is always sunny. Then there is no question. Or in Seattle or Oxford, which (alas) have the opposite problem.

8. Matthew 12:23 (ESV).

9. In this instance, the Pharisees try to close that gap by answering the people's question for them, but Jesus rejects their attempt and leaves it open.

standable reasons. Children are naturally inquisitive: they search and explore their surroundings with abandon. The university is, for many of us, one of the last seasons of intentional questioning. And these days, many young people broadcast their doubts, which I understand but try to avoid.

But if the young question most, the wise question best.[10] The art of questioning takes a lifetime to perfect, for the most interesting questions flow from a deep well of insights. The more we understand, the more fine-grained our awareness of the negative spaces will be. The more we learn about the world, the more we will realize how much more there is to know, if we will only remember our ignorance and continue noticing the negative spaces. Those who have learned best and longest will explore hidden nooks and corners that those of us starting out cannot begin to imagine. The wise have seen negative spaces that only well-trained eyes are strong enough to detect.

IMAGINING AND THE VALUE OF QUESTIONS

What shall we say about Job, the most famous of the Bible's questioners? Having lost everything, he bitterly laments his state while fending off the bad advice from friends that he should confess his wrongdoing. Job's sense of injustice reveals itself in his pointed questioning of God about his sorrows. "Does it seem to you good to oppress, to despise the work of your hands and favor the designs of the wicked? Have you eyes of flesh? Do you see as man sees?"[11] But his inquiries are never answered; instead, they are subverted and chastened. God speaks from the whirlwind and returns to Job a barrage of His own questions that expose Job's

---

10. This is why many wise people seem so "young at heart." Questioning makes the world feel new, which is partly why it is a youthful activity and so difficult to maintain as we grow old.

11. Job 10:3–4 (ESV).

limited power and understanding. While Job asks God whether He has the eyes of a man, God retorts by wondering whether Job has the eyes of God.

G. K. Chesterton famously wrote of that conclusion that the "riddles of God are more satisfying than the answers of man," and there's something to his point.[12] Certainly the riddles of the book of Job are more satisfying than most interpretations of it. God throws His questions about like lightning and thunder, with a sarcastic bite that is terrifying: "Where were you when I laid the foundation of the earth? Tell me, if you have understanding. Who determined its measurements—surely you know! Or who stretched the line upon it? On what were its bases sunk, or who laid its cornerstone, when the morning stars sang together and all the sons of God shouted for joy?"[13]

The effect of God's response is impossible to summarize. To simply say, as I did above, that God transcends our understanding reduces the point to banality and keeps us at a safe distance from its power. God's questions are invitations to explore the gap between God and creation from within. When God asks, "Have you entered into the springs of the sea or walked in the recesses of the deep?" there is no doubt about the answer. But by using questions, God invites Job to look at creation as He does so Job can see the gap for himself. God's questions are a form of saying "come and see," rather than a didactic exposition on the nature of God's uniqueness and incomprehensibility.

God's questions help Job reimagine his world in order to more clearly see his place within it, a place that is surrounded by a host of unknowns. They take Job beyond staring into the void and keep him from losing himself amidst a sea of negations or denials.

---

12. G. K. Chesterton, *Introduction to the Book of Job*. Available at the American Chesterton Society (www.chesterton.org).

13. Job 38:4–7 (ESV).

Job is taken beyond simply loving the "negative spaces" for their own sake. Each time he is confronted by a question, he comes face-to-face with God. Job has not "entered into the springs of the sea," but in recognizing this gap in his knowledge Job is confronted by the one who has. The questions themselves help Job understand himself and God more clearly—himself in the light of God—which is why Job will respond to God that he has now seen Him face-to-face. [14]

It is through imaginative deliberation that we are able to make sense of God's questions. What does it mean for Job to "walk in the recesses of the deep"? Understanding the question depends upon conceiving its terms, which takes us beyond the naked confrontation with an abstract question and into the act of exploring and searching out. We imagine a world that both explains the question and might provide an answer—much like we do when looking for the right piece for our puzzle. We look at both our existing picture and the pieces before us and turn and test each possibility to discern how and where they belong. The question opens a "negative space" before us—but as we search out its meaning, the negative space both illuminates and clarifies everything else, helping us to see.

THE BEGINNING OF OUR QUESTIONS

Where do questions come from? That's an odd way of putting it, I realize, but the impulse to inquire about the world is an odd phenomenon. We feel the presence of unknowns; we notice the negative spaces. And we set about exploring because we feel, however opaquely, that what we discover will be good. We believe that our finding will be better than for the unknown to remain unknown, that our apprehending the truth will somehow make us whole. The good and the true go together. As theologian

---

14. Job 42:5 (ESV).

Thomas Aquinas put it, "truth is something good, otherwise it would not be desirable; and good is something true, otherwise it would not be intelligible." When we relate to the unknown, though, goodness goes before and beyond the truth. Our belief that the truth will be good *even when* we don't know it moves us to search and inquire. Why would we search out the world if we did not think that what we find would be better for us? The love of goodness precedes our knowledge and stands beneath and within all of our exploring.

Because questioning is a form that our love takes, it is a practice that demands more of us than our intellects. In a passage that has become something of an anthem for younger Christians eager to embrace a questioning life, poet Rainer Maria Rilke writes:

> You're so young, so far from any beginning; I should like to ask you, dear sir, as well as I can, to show patience towards everything in your heart that has not been resolved and to try to cherish *the questions themselves*, like sealed rooms and books written in a language that is very foreign. Do not hunt for the answers just now—they cannot be given to you because you cannot live them. What matters is that you live everything. And you must now *live* the questions. One day perhaps you will gradually and imperceptibly live your way into the answer.[15]

Questioning well is not a task to be marked off in our plan for self-improvement. It has no formula to apply, no technique that can be mastered. It is a form of life, a practice that encompasses and entangles our hearts, minds, and bodies. Which means that we will live ourselves into the answers only if we live the questions well, orienting them around the good and the true that are

---

15. Rainer Maria Rilke, *Letters to a Young Poet*, trans. Mark Harman (Cambridge, MA: Harvard University Press, 2011), 45–46.

revealed in the person of Jesus.

The sort of questions that we *can* live arise when we linger over our lives, when we patiently and deliberately peer into unknown corners with the boundless, childlike energy of those eager to discover what all shall be. They bubble up from our communities and the challenges we face to live well within them. They land in front of us, when societies move away from convictions they once took for granted. Marriage, monogamy, the need for two parents—these are no longer assumed as they once were. We take up our questions when we are taken up *by* them. The inquiries that we make reveal ourselves and our commitments, for as expressions of our loves they signify what we care most about.

This is why questions rise to the surface during seasons of suffering, even if the suffering is not our own. Pain renders the world's goodness *questionable*. It shocks us out of our complacent attachment to the blessings of comfort and prosperity. It reopens the universe to us, casting a shadow over our lives and the goodness we had wrongly "taken for granted." When we see the reason for our pain, when we are finally given the meaning—the satisfaction will be a joy beyond words, a peace beyond understanding. But until then, the questions that grip us demonstrate the nature of our hearts and our fundamental need for the purification of our desires.

It is a sign of the frailty of contemporary Christianity, rather than its strength, that we often do not begin to question until the megaphone of suffering has awakened us from our sleep. Until suffering comes upon us, the explorations that consume our hearts and our communities reflect the shallowness of our lives. We ask our questions forgetting that we lie under the shadow—under the sentence—of death. Our lack of courage keeps us free to live among distractions and trivialities and stay within the warm comfort of our own understanding. But our "freedom" is only bondage, and these days our chains are only broken when death and pain's rude irruption turns our faces toward the unknown, undiscovered country all around us.

LEARNING TO LIVE THE RIGHT QUESTIONS

If I may add to the distinguished poet, I would suggest that we not only "live the questions" but consider which questions we should live. We may care about a question because it is ours, but that is simply to suffer from an (un)natural vanity. It is the starting place, but we cannot stay there. For if we are to enter into the questioning life, we might begin by questioning ourselves. Not all our inquiries deserve the time and attention we are inclined to give them. We ought not give ourselves the benefit of the doubt if we plan on doubting everything else. Both our lives and their questions must be placed on the altar, tested, and tried to discern whether they will last until the end of all things.

We can learn to ask better questions. We read old books to learn to ask the questions of those who have gone before us. And we read the *great* books because the questions they pose go into the center of things, even if the answers they put forward and the worlds they imagine are not always true. And we read Scripture to see the questions that arise from it, to learn to see the hidden spaces of the world from the vantage point of God and man.

Questioning well takes a whole life. We don't wake and master the practice in a morning. When I taught the occasional class at the Torrey Honors Institute—an educational environment that inculcates habits of excellent questioning—the difference between the freshmen and seniors was striking. Something happens in the hundreds of hours of practice that helps students ask better questions on the far side. Like any endeavor, inquiry has its own rules and norms. It's possible to inquire badly, just as it's possible

to play piano badly. And we learn those norms as we learn anything else: by studying, imitating, and practicing.

As someone who loves questioning, I am well acquainted
with the internal defensiveness that arises at the suggestion that
my questions are badly conceived, or badly timed, or asked with an
impure intention. Surely we speak only of other people and their
errant inquiries! But the possibility of questioning badly is what
makes questioning so interesting, if perilous. In the long journey
into understanding, a misstep really matters and a wrong turn
might place us in danger. It is the sort of life-and-death stuff that
every true adventure hangs on.

It is possible for our exploring to imperceptibly lead us toward destinations we never imagined at the outset. Our questions
can quietly assume the tenor of demands, such that we would pull
the Almighty down to us and compel Him to answer. Or we can
treat them as bricks in our towers, as was built at Babel, as we
scale the heights in comic acts of hubris. Searching the nooks and
crannies is not for the faint of heart. "Guard your steps," the author of Ecclesiastes writes, "when you go to the house of God." [16]
We shouldn't be so naive as to think it safe to explore things into
which angels long to look.

We like to speak of those who "make the faith their own,"
which has now become something of a rite of passage within
the North American church. Such a process sometimes involves
leaving—imaginatively, at least—our fathers' house and exploring
paths that we suspect might lead to a more flourishing environment. And sometimes such explorations actually do take us in
new and surprising directions. For we do not all start with the
truth. Nor do all of us end with it.

But to begin that journey is to play the prodigal. Raising ques-

---

16. Ecclesiatstes 5:1 (ESV).

tions about our communities' presuppositions or their most cherished beliefs is not necessarily transgressive, but it can certainly feel that way.[17] It is commendable to search out and explore the doctrine of the Trinity, to come up to the brink of our own understanding. But those around us who have never been taken up by questions may struggle to distinguish between questioning and denial, making them react to our inquiries with suspicion and fear. The life of exploring is a different sort of life, and it takes everyone a little time to get used to. In waking to the strangeness of the world, many of us become strangers in our own homes.

But home is where we start and where we shall someday return. The path between has been marked out for us by a Savior who became the prodigal from heaven, journeying into the far country to bring us home with Him. He is both the end of our exploring and its liberating transformation. It is Jesus who has already profaned the mysteries of God by making the unknown at the center known to us: he who has seen Jesus has seen the Father. "Although [wisdom] is actually our homeland," St. Augustine once said, "it has also made itself the road to our homeland."[18] The beginning of questioning well is to *seek to question well*, which may mean laying down our questions and allowing them to be reshaped and reformed by the answers given us by God. For if Christianity is true, then the end of our exploring will be joy and goodness and life. But the path leads down the *via Dolorosa* and up toward Golgotha, as we take up our cross and follow the One who went ahead.

---

17. And sometimes, it is. There is a time and a place for everything and a necessary limit on our questioning that we should respect.

18. Augustine and R. P. H. Green, *On Christian Teaching* (Oxford, England; New York: Oxford University Press, 1999), 13.

2

When the Questions
Are Not Neutral

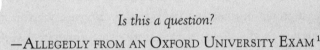

The role of a witness during a trial seems fairly straightforward, at least from the outside. The lawyer asks a question that the witness answers. Having seen this process unfold countless times on TV, it seemed to me that answering truthfully would be especially easy if there's nothing personal at stake. How hard could it be to describe what we have witnessed? As it turns out, a good deal more difficult than it appears.

I have been deposed once in my life, and by the time it was done I vowed it wouldn't happen again.[2] I had witnessed a car crash that I later learned had tragically left its only victim a quadriplegic. A mother of two children on her way to work was speeding down the freeway when her rear tire blew out. Her car skidded off the road

---

1. Colin Dexter, *Death Is Now My Neighbor: An Inspector Morse Novel* (New York: Crown Publishers, 1996), 388.

2. I mean, if I could help it. Some unpleasantries are unavoidable.

and bounced down an embankment. One moment she was there and the next she was gone. Some fifty people stopped to help, and when the police came I told them what I had seen.

A year later, I found myself fifty floors up in the Wilshire Building in downtown Los Angeles. Injury lawyers had helped the woman sue the tire maker, car manufacturer, the mechanics who did her car maintenance, and God Himself. When I walked in, I noticed three investigators delicately putting the shredded tire back together. They were preparing for a long, drawn out affair.

My part was supposed to be simple: get in, answer the questions, and get out. Instead, I underwent three exhausting hours of questioning and cross-examination by lawyers who fit the stereotypes to the point of caricature. The corporate lawyers had recently graduated from top-tier law schools and worked in downtown Chicago. They carried themselves with the sort of stiff, upper-class professionalism that made it very clear that they were good and that they knew it. The injury lawyers were from a small firm in Kansas City and had the sort of smarmy, easygoing overconfidence of the daytime ambulance chaser crowd.

Even though the deposition happened a full year after the wreck, I walked in confident of my story. One doesn't simply forget seeing a car disappear from the road. But by the time the Chicago lawyers were finished with me, the only reason I had to believe that anything had happened at all was that shredded tire being meticulously rebuilt in the room next door. The opening exchange with team Chicago went something like this:

> "Tell us what you saw that day."
>
> "Well, the car in question passed me and then the tire blew out. I . . ."

"Blew out? What do you mean by that?"

(stunned silence)

"Um, uh, well, it came apart."

"It went flat?"

"Not exactly. I had to dodge pieces."

"So it disintegrated."

"Well, no. I mean, disintegration is a strong word for something that comes apart. It ... er ... well ..."

And so on. Turns out, describing what happens when a tire "blows out" is really hard work. That sort of rigorous dissecting went on for two hours, leaving me feeling totally muddled.

Then it was team Kansas City's turn. They took the vaguest, broadest approach possible. "Where did the car end up?" "Was the tire still working?" Details apparently weren't their thing. The whole episode ended with a bang, as they asked me whether I was doing anything else while driving.

"Yes," I told them. "I was talking with my wife. We were discussing putting new tires on our car."

The lawyers' questions weren't neutral. Each legal team had an objective and their questions were worded accordingly. Their inquiries served one fundamental goal: winning. They didn't care about understanding what happened that day, and the truth was of secondary importance. Each team needed my testimony to help their case. As questioners, they were masters of the craft: they knew that the way they framed their inquiries, the points that they pressed or chose to ignore, would draw out details that would help their case while neglecting the parts that wouldn't.

Our questions are more like the lawyers' than we realize. They come *from* somewhere and *take* us somewhere. They slant our perspectives in particular directions and make some answers more plausible than others. While we might like to exonerate ourselves from the burden of responsibility for them, in the long exploration into the world around us, there are no neutral questions.

THE FIRST QUESTION WAS NOT GOD'S AND IT WAS NOT GOOD

"Did God actually say, 'You shall not eat of any tree in the garden'?" So the serpent asks Adam and Eve in Genesis 3. It seems like such an innocent question and about such a simple matter, almost like asking, "What did you see on the interstate that day?" Answer and move on, respond and keep living. Or so it seems. Read carefully, though, and things turn out to be more complex.

The question inaugurates a new stage for Adam and Eve. To that point in the story, they had not encountered anything that would call into question the trustworthiness of God's command. Their obedience had been straightforward and direct, as they apparently had never needed it to be anything else. "God said it, I believe it, that settles it," the cliché goes. That sort of naïve commitment might be troubling these days, but only because it is a perversion of a genuine good. There is something commendable about a devout simplicity, something beautiful about an eager willingness to obey without question once a gracious commandment has been given. After all, the serpent isn't the hero of the story, and if God did in fact "say it," could there a *better* reason to believe it?

The only path beyond questions that are posed to us requires going through them. A question claims our attention; it directs our mental gaze toward a particular feature of the world. Adam and Eve could have ignored the serpent's question. But such a conscious decision can only be made by acknowledging the question's intrinsic power. Had Adam and Eve fled the scene, they still would have taken with them the new awareness that questions *could* be asked.

This new awareness is a double-edged sword. On the one hand, by calling into question God's command, the serpent made space for a more critical, reflective obedience—a deeper trust, if you will. Adam and Eve would still have been responsible to "trust and obey," but they would do both, knowing that their obedience was not a *given*. Their faithfulness could no longer be assumed: in the face of the serpent's question, it must now be demonstrated.

On the other hand, the serpent's question was designed to erode Adam and Eve's trust in the gracious providence of God. Rather than make open warfare, the serpent cloaks his resistance in the innocent garb of inquiry. "Did God *actually* say?" It carries a note of disbelief, of uncertainty and hesitation, about God's command. It is suggestive and provocative not because it is edgy but because the serpent has a point: the goodness of God's revelation isn't quite so straightforward as Adam and Eve initially believed.

Not content with a single assault, though, the serpent opens up multiple fronts. The name he uses for God subtly drives a wedge between Adam and Eve and their Creator. The only name the text uses for God to that point is *YHWH*, the "Lord God," the one who is near to His people and will remain faithful to them. But the serpent switches to the more generic name *Elohim*, replacing the intimate, gracious authoritarianism of *the Lord God* with a more distant conception of deity akin to the "man upstairs." It seems like a minor change, but it moves Adam and Eve into foreign and less friendly territory.

And then there is the most obvious fault in the serpent's question: God did not *actually* say, "You shall not eat of any tree in the garden." He did not say that at all. The quotation is a misquotation, a bit of bad scholarship. It will not be the last time in Scripture Satan (deliberately) misreads God's commands, which ought to be

a cautionary tale for us all.[3] And the freedom the serpent promises is only effective because his reading is that of a dour legalist.
Where God grants permission—"You may surely eat of every tree
of the garden," save only the one—the serpent sees only restric-
tion. Adam and Eve had been placed in a paradise of pleasures,
none of which the serpent was fit to enjoy.

In recent years, we have been repeatedly reminded that the
medium is the message, that the form of our content is an intrinsic
part of its meaning. In this instance, the inquiry has a fatal flaw.
It redraws the boundaries God established and casts aspersions
on God's character. The question itself casts a shadow over the
Lord God and His kindness, a shadow that becomes the shadow
of death.

Unfaithful Questioning

The man who asks whether God's mercy allows for justice
may be asking a sincere question and faithfully opening himself to
the creative destruction of his own false ideas or to a deepened
understanding of his true ones.[4] His questioning may be rooted in
love and aimed at his growth. Or he may be clinging to the final
vestiges of his rebellion, making a final desperate stand against the
holiness of God. Or he may be merely playing a game, reducing
God to an abstraction for his own intellectual satisfaction. These
possibilities and countless others stand beneath every inquiry
that we make.

How can we tell if our questions are subverting the healthy
confidence that we or others have in God? How do we know if we

---

3. See the confrontation between Jesus and Satan in the wilderness in Matthew
   4:1–11.

4. It is a mistake here to speak of "his" ideas at all. Ideas cannot be possessed. See:
   Paul J. Griffiths, *Intellectual Appetite: A Theological Grammar* (Washington, DC:
   Catholic University of America Press, 2009).

have deceived ourselves into believing we are "just questioning" rather than expressing our hostility against God, a hostility that may even be hidden from ourselves? That such self-deceived rationalizations of our questions are a possibility should be enough to give us pause. It is a serious thing we undertake, this exploring.

There can be no "merely" or "just" of our questioning. Such qualifiers indicate that we think our inquiries are somehow exempt from sin and temptation. It would be convenient to think that our questions are immune from the fundamental conflict of right and wrong, that they are quarantined from the possibility of confession and repentance. But the first moment of questioning well is the recognition that as a human endeavor, our questioning is fallen and broken, entangled with sin and in need of reformation. We should be wary of affording to ourselves a cheap grace that cordons off a crucial area of our lives from our responsibility before God.

Of course, the instinctive reaction to the possibility that we are questioning badly is to raise up the defenses. We presuppose that because our questions are sincerely asked, our sincerity is enough. Not many of our questions are consciously subversive the way the serpent's was. But the serpent's question was also a badly *worded* question. The form itself, not just the intention, was broken. And while the sincerity of our intentions is always open to scrutiny, so too is the form of our questions. We can only know the quality of our own inquiries after we examine them. The faithfulness of our questioning simply cannot be assumed.

To put it differently, the person who wonders, "Where were you while we suffered?" might be making known to God the depths of his heartbreak without demanding from Him an answer. The question may be asked as a way of expressing a patient desire to understand the ways and purposes of God, of longing exploring with a faith striving to see. But he might also pose the question belligerently, defiantly implying that God failed in His duties. Or he may be procrastinating, retreating into a difficult intellectual pursuit in order to escape the weightiness of suffering, lest it overwhelm him. He may in fact pose the question thinking it rooted in his faithfulness to God and only discover later the latent and undiscovered brokenness of his heart. There are a thousand ways our questioning can go wrong but generally very few in which it can go right.

As long as we live beneath the shadow, we must consider the possibility that the desires and motivations beneath our questions will be hidden even from ourselves. I have sometimes thought that it is our capacity for self-deception that marks us off as human. We are more skilled at hiding from our own gaze than we realize and more eager to give ourselves the benefit of the doubt than we should be. And so those who are prone to question must, above all, question themselves.[5] As long as we consider our questions outside the realm of sin and sanctification, we establish them as idols, ironically creating the conditions for our own spiritual and intellectual frustration.

Questioning is not a safe practice, nor is self-justifying. The mere fact that we are questioning does not mean we should be or that we should be questioning *in that way*. How should we then question? When should we ask a question? How shall we frame our question? What shall we question for? To whom shall we pose our questions and when shall we ask them? We cannot simply go forward on the assumption we have those questions truly answered. For we may raise our questioning itself up against the knowledge of God.

---

5. Such self-inquiry does not need to be obsessive, nor overly introspective. "Acquit me from hidden faults!" is the cry, and quick repentance is our prayer. If things are amiss, God will show them to us. And if God doesn't, well, carry on.

QUESTIONING OUR QUESTIONS —AND OURSELVES

The first thing to ask when our faith is "called into question," as Adam and Eve's was, is whether the inquiry is an invitation to join the rebellion. Does the form of the question itself presuppose hostility toward God? Is it the sort of question slanted toward our faithful obedience or toward the hostility of rebellion? Eve's failure to detect the serpent's sly shifting of categories put her at an immediate disadvantage. She failed to question both the question and the questioner. But if we wish not merely to question but to question well, we need to become more attentive to the forms inquiries take.[6]

Eve, for example, might have pushed back at the wording of the serpent's inquiry to expose the question's false foundations. "Why is it that you have changed the name for God? Why have you misquoted Him?" Responding to the serpent's disingenuous questions with inquiries of her own might have drawn to the surface its veiled hostility against the Creator. In Matthew 22, when the Pharisees ask Jesus whether it is lawful to pay taxes, Jesus brings to the surface their "malice" by asking why they are putting Him to the test.[7] By responding to questions with other questions, we learn to see the more fundamental concerns and desires that often lie beneath inquiries.

Or Eve might have momentarily accepted the terms of debate the serpent offered in order to imaginatively construct the world in a way that made the serpent's question intelligible and its fruit

---

6. I do not mean simply the linguistic form. Though I have not the room to dig up all the details here, the meaning of questions seems to hinge upon both the linguistic form and the intention of the asker. Sometimes we ask questions we do not "mean" to ask, which are opportunities for learning and growth.

7. Matthew 22:15–22 (ESV).

(death) clear. She nearly does this, but without the intentionality of exploring the world of the serpent's question. She keeps the more distant name for God and misquotes God's command. Both of these revisions make her final rebellion more plausible as an outcome. But those are bad answers to a bad question, rather than an exploration of the world behind the question itself. What difference does it make whether God is intimate or far off? What sort of world would it be if He had actually commanded them to "not eat of any tree in the garden?" The serpent's question leads to death because it originates in a false picture of the world.

Imaginative exploration of this sort is not itself sin.[8] One can consider an action without thereby desiring it or intending it. A detective may have to imagine himself as a thief in order to better understand the crime. And we all read novels about murder without ourselves committing murder. We imaginatively step into false pictures of the world when we watch movies or go to plays. And in doing so we learn to see the wages of sin and desire it less.[9] But despite the potential gain, we ought only take this path with some fear and trembling. Imaginative constructions can disorder our desires that, if left unreformed, will blossom into the deadness of sin.

Entering into false questions and dialogues with those who ask them is a dangerous and frequently fruitless activity. So it's easy to think Adam and Eve would have been better off to simply go about their business. But that would be to deny a native desire to understand what we have been given, to see the meaning beneath the commands that we obey.

It is precisely this dangerous path C. S. Lewis marks out in *Perelandra*, his fanciful retelling of the Bible's creation narrative.

---

8. It would be sin to imagine ourselves engaging in acts of sin for the purposes of feeling some minor satisfaction from our fantasies. But that is a different case.

9. Though I hasten to add that such lessons are not the point of reading fiction or seeing movies or what have you.

Lewis's Eve character enters into a dialogue with her antagonistic foe and adopts a way of viewing the world that is hostile to her Creator. Lewis's story ends very differently than the biblical story, with Eve escaping temptation and remaining obedient. Yet it is not her skill with words or her intellectual prowess that helps her escape but a third party who uses brute force. Even so, in her summation she points out that she learned something through her faithfulness that she would not have gained had she disobeyed:

> We have learned of evil, though not as the Evil One wanted us to learn. We have learned better than that and know it more, for it is waking that understands sleep and not sleep that understands waking. There is an ignorance of evil that comes from being young: there is a darker ignorance that comes from doing it, as man by sleeping loses knowledge of sleep.[10]

This is a point worth underlining, as it is popular to presume that we can't understand a struggle or question unless we have wrestled with it ourselves. That may be true in some cases, but not so with sin: it is Jesus who understands the outer reaches of temptation because He resisted until the end. He is able to see our sin perfectly precisely because He hasn't any. Sin clouds things up, makes the intellectual vision bend sideways. While we tend to privilege the "authentic" testimony of those who struggle, understanding comes to those who remain innocent of evil without remaining ignorant of it.

Of course, Lewis's Eve resolves her questions. And so must we all, even if that means coming to see why the questions themselves were the wrong ones to ask. Questions designed to unsettle us cannot be ignored—at least not for very long. And they can only be satisfied by our entering into a deeper understanding of

10. C. S. Lewis, *Perelandra* (London: Pan Books, 1953).

the goodness of God and of His creation. For unless they are eventually diagnosed and replaced with more faithful inquiries, such questions will rot into the bitterness of rebellion.

THE REDEMPTION OF QUESTIONING AND THE QUESTIONS OF REDEMPTION

The terror of authority that accompanies a guilty conscience can be devastating. I was in fifth grade when I felt it with a sharpness that has stayed with me. I decided against reason and good sense to join with a group of boys in repeatedly throwing a wet Nerf football at a classmate. Brilliant fellows that we were, we didn't choose just any girl: we picked the principal's daughter. It was bullying, plain and simple, and I am still sorry for it. But the moment I was sent to the principal's office, I knew I was done for. My knees haven't knocked much in this life, but they were at it hard then.

It's a poignant memory for me, and it stacks up alongside several others from those years of life. The purity of my terror and the fear associated with the conscious realization that I *was wrong*—the stark clarity of those sensations still amazes me. As I have grown, it's interesting how opaque and complex my feelings have become. The wrongs I do now seem more ambiguous and the authorities not quite as obvious.

I may be betraying my immaturity by noting it, but it is easy in our self-determining, self-aggrandizing age to forget how to view the world through the lens of obedience and disobedience. The lines between obedience and disobedience, right and wrong, grow harder to grasp once the moral criterion shifts away from being tied to the approval or shame of our parents. [11] That distance changes our confrontation with our own sin: while the pangs of

---

11. This is, I suspect, largely cultural. Honor and shame in other cultures are major means of motivating behavior. Less so for us.

conscience may still be around, they are less obviously tied to an awareness that beneath the wrong is an authority whose commandment we have broken.[12]

Adam and Eve had no mediation of memory or time or the world to stand between them and God. They had received the command in all its starkness and presumably had grasped its meaning. They had no reason to question the trustworthiness of the command or of the one who had given it. But once the serpent muddies the water, the decision to obey takes shape against the possibility of disobedience and their understanding of God takes on a good deal more importance.

Tragically, they swallow the serpent's bait and die on his hook. Rather than face up to their transgression, they stitch together clothing and trundle off into the woods in their hurry to avoid being found out. It is not God who makes Himself into a question but they. And it is not God who hides Himself but they who flee from Him. It is His presence they cannot abide, for their sin has transformed the good into a horror. The open question of their faithful obedience is transformed into the open question of God's response: Will He extend mercy in the midst of His judgment? But rather than stand before the unknown and take their lumps, they choose the path of procrastinating avoidance.

God's first word to them is not an offer of forgiveness, though, or the verdict of punishment. It is a question. While the rebellion of man against God was launched with a convoluted, poorly worded query, the rebellion of God against sin takes a simpler, more powerful form: "Where are you?"[13]

It's a perplexing thing that an omniscient God would ask a question. Certainly He knows where they are. Yet the question

---

12. Mostly, we think about wrongs in terms of harms we cause other people. Or goods that we fail to fulfill. Those are both appropriate, but may not be sufficient.

13. Genesis 3:9 (ESV).

expresses an interest in Adam and Eve. Even from the beginning, in the moment of our sin, God does not want only to be Lord over us but God with and among us. Relationships demand mutual self-disclosure. Both parties open themselves to the other through speaking and listening. And in that exchange, they momentarily stand on the same plane, meeting and welcoming each other. Even disagreement demands a shared intellectual place; otherwise people simply find each other incomprehensible. By posing a question, God moves toward Adam and Eve and gives them the opportunity to speak with Him. His question rebuilds the ground between them that their sin had ruptured.

God's question is the starting point for their journey of return. It is an invitation, and as a word of God to man, it is a moment of grace. It is the first moment of God's redemptive activity: in asking, God reminds us that He will listen as we speak, even if we utter a confession. And the question helps Adam and Eve find themselves by acknowledging where they had gone to. We can only begin our journey from where we are, *but most of us don't even know where we are.* Identifying our emotional, mental, and spiritual surroundings proves more difficult than it might seem—as I suspect any counselor would readily affirm. Things on the surface seem so simple, as they did for me in the lawyer's office. We think we know all that we have done and seen. But when God asks His questions, we are left to confess the makeshift and hasty nature of our garments.

Sin is a condition of lostness, the condition of not being able to find ourselves because we have turned from the One from whom all distances are measured. And in its worst form, it is the condition of our being lost *without realizing* that we happen to be lost. By rebelling against God, we move Him to the margins, breaking our relationship with ourselves and the world. But it is easy to forget our condition, to enter into a slumber and sleepwalk through our lives.

We can only begin to make our way back home if we open ourselves to the questions God has for us. Just as Dante's epic poem *The Divine Comedy* begins with him waking to find himself lost in a dark wood—a curious phenomenon, for how can one awake and find himself lost?—so the first step of return begins when we recognize and say that we too have gone astray. We begin from where we are, even if we start from nowhere. "To return to the place where we are not, we must go through the way in which we are not,"[14] is T. S. Eliot's lovely phrase. The only return toward God is by acknowledging we have departed, a fact that God already knows but desires us to utter all the same.

This dialogue of confession has its own dangers, of course. It is just as easy to justify ourselves through it, to use the fact that we are now speaking to avoid the burden of admitting our guilt. God's second question to Adam—"Who told you that you were naked?"—is met with Adam's subtle redirection away from himself and toward Eve. "The woman whom you gave to be with me, she gave me fruit of the tree, and I ate."[15] Adam resorts to overliteralism as he attempts to escape responsibility on a technicality.

The path toward questioning well demands that we surrender ourselves to the questions of God and make our confession if necessary. Or to put it another way, the true beginning of our exploring is when we are explored by God. Inquiry stands under judgment: it is a gracious judgment, to be sure, by a judge whose mercy is everlasting. But the quality of God's mercy can only be known through the corresponding repentance of our sin. And if we think we can explore the foundations of our own questions and the reasons of our own hearts without deepening our own

---

14. Eliot, *Four Quartets*, 17.
15. Genesis 3:11–12 (ESV).

self-deception and self-justification, then our vanity is more pervasive than we realize. The psalmist's prayer is that God would search his heart, that all his hidden ways would be known.[16] Just as the deepest moments of our prayers are accessible only to the indwelling Holy Spirit, so the depths of our sin will remain hidden to us until Jesus mercifully finds them out.[17]

Opening ourselves to being questioned by God means, here and now, surrendering ourselves to the Word of Scripture, a word that probes and questions us as we read it. As many questions as we have about the world and as important as they are, we should remember that the Bible has its own questions that it poses to us. Will we faithfully strive to understand the text? Will we live within its commandments, once we discern them? How shall we respond when Jesus asks, "And who do you say I am?" "Do you take offense at this?" "Do you want to go away as well?"[18] Learning to ask questions along with Scripture means opening ourselves to the text, integrating it into our hearts and habits, and allowing it to reform our inquiries.

Remaining open to the questions of God is at the heart of walking in faith and trusting in His goodness despite the terror we might feel. If we have known pain and injustice at the hands of authority, then those who abused us will have their reward, in this life, the next, or both. As for us, we are safe in the hands of God, even if such safety someday means the death of ourselves and all we know. But we can only welcome those questions we first open our ears to hear, and I worry that these days we are so noisily putting forth our own questions that we have no silence to listen to His.

---

16. Psalm 19:12 (ESV).

17. And God will allow them to stay hidden from us, until we are ready to see them, as a manifestation of His grace. For more, see Gregg A. Ten Elshof, *I Told Me So: Self-Deception and the Christian Life* (Grand Rapids: Eerdmans, 2009).

18. Matthew 16:15; John 6:61; John 6:67 (ESV).

3

On Doubt and
What Doubt Isn't

You say you didn't mean any harm; did you mean any good, Curdie? —GEORGE MACDONALD[1]

Though I have spent little of my life on it, I have long been fascinated by the sea. For many, the ocean has been domesticated: it is nothing except the massive blue expanse beneath our airplanes or the backdrop for our holidays. In the Pacific Northwest, where I was raised, the ocean does not have the allure of quiet waves. Nor is it a place for the fun and recreation of swimming and surfing, at least not for the sane. Its beauty is darker and more menacing, and its fundamental power has not been forgotten. The sea has a cruel goodness, for it takes life even while providing it, as those who live near it can unhappily attest.

What the emptiness of space was for the post–World War II era, the sea was for much of the rest of our history. It was a dangerous, infinite expanse, a territory that cartographers would

---

1. George MacDonald, *The Princess and Curdie* (Glasgow: Blackie & Son, 1888), 25.

guess about but could not explore. In the world of the Bible, ships would hug the shore because the open water was perilous. We have long forgotten why men would sacrifice to the gods before embarking. Safe passage has not always been the certainty it is for us today.

Our distance from the sea and its ancient meaning makes it hard to resonate with Paul's most impressive mixed metaphors in Ephesians 4:13–14. The ministries of the church, Paul suggests, are aimed at building us up "to mature manhood, the measure of the stature of the fullness of Christ." He contrasts this with children who are "tossed to and fro by the waves and carried about by every wind of doctrine." The image is a strange one, simultaneously evoking amusement and horror.

But his point is straightforward: maturity is a kind of stability, a steadfastness. The complete person is as unmoved as God. He has a fixity to him, a surety that the chaos of a fallen world cannot touch him at the center. "My anchor holds within the veil," the old song puts it.[2] That anchor may be tested—*will* be tested—if we walk with Jesus. But those who are mature know that it holds, that their position is secure. "[The Lord's] steadfast love endures forever" is the promise, and it shows up often enough in the Psalms to ensure we don't miss the point.

But our experience of the Christian life is often neither smooth nor straightforward. Many of us are more familiar with a sort of hesitating, unsteady affirmation of the faith than we are with the quiet confidence of those who rest secure. Sometimes our belief hangs by a thread. It is not Paul's bold affirmations that resonate with us but the desperate prayer of the man who wanted his son to be healed: "Lord, I believe; help my unbelief!"[3] The mo-

2. Edward Mote, "My Hope Is Built on Nothing Less", circa 1834; first appeared in Mote's *Hymns of Praise*, 1836.

3. Mark 9:24 (NKJV).

ments of assurance we experience are often overshadowed by the vague instability of doubt.

Christians have spoken in the past of faith as a virtue, which is a good way to think about it. It comes to us as a gift. It cannot be earned. But like all gifts, it must be cherished and cultivated if it is to flourish and endure. The land God gives Israel as an inheritance must be claimed and all of its enemy occupants eventually driven out. So the faith that works our salvation sometimes must be buttressed against withering attacks of doubt. From the earliest moment I can remember in the church, the apostle Peter's willingness to race across a raging sea to see Jesus has been put forward as the paradigm of faithful obedience. And for very good reason. The eager recognition of God in Jesus Christ often takes us across and beyond places that others tremble to go. We are surrounded on every side by dangers, which we would be foolish to ignore.

THE CULTURAL VIRTUE OF DOUBT

René Descartes wanted certainty. That is the story we are often told and it is true enough. He was a philosopher in the seventeenth century and is often blamed for inaugurating a "rationalistic" approach to the world. To arrive at certainty, Descartes systematized his skepticism. By doing so he sowed the wind, and we are still reaping the whirlwind. His emphasis on certainty is often treated as one of the hallmarks of "modernism," which we have now gone beyond with our "postmodern" suspicions and recognition of limitations. But the paradox is that there are few more "modern" approaches to the world than to doubt what we have received from tradition and authority. In its popular form, postmodern doubt is merely modern skepticism with hipster glasses.

The one rule of our current intellectual climate, in fact, is that we should doubt everything first. Only then, if it is somehow left standing at the end, should we go on to believe it. As Wayne Booth put it:

> [Our contemporary dogma] teaches that we have no justification for asserting what can be doubted, and we are commanded by it to doubt whatever cannot be proved. In that view one never is advised to see the capacity for belief as an intellectual virtue. Though few have ever put it quite so bluntly as the young [Bertrand] Russell in his more prophetic moments, to doubt is taken as the supreme achievement of thought.[4]

Or as Booth wrote elsewhere, the modern dogma is that "the job of thought is to doubt whatever can be doubted."

Wayne Booth wrote that in 1974. But a century before him, philosopher Søren Kierkegaard summed up the intellectual mood of his day this way:

> What those ancient Greeks, who also surely understood a little about philosophy, assumed to be a task for the whole lifetime, because proficiency in doubt is not achieved in a matter of days and weeks; what was achieved by the old veteran polemicist [Descartes], who had preserved the equilibrium of doubt through all specious arguments . . . with that everyone in our age *begins.*[5]

That's not exactly a compliment. Kierkegaard's concern is that making doubt the posture from which we interact with the world inadvertently trivializes and cheapens it. Doubt is too valu-

---

4. Wayne C. Booth, *Modern Dogma and the Rhetoric of Assent* (Notre Dame, IN: University of Notre Dame Press, 1974), 101. This is a great book. And "contemporary" doesn't simply mean in the 1970s.

5. Søren Kierkegaard, Stephen Evans, and Sylvia Walsh, *Fear and Trembling* (New York: Cambridge University Press, 2006), 4. The emphasis at the end is mine. And for whatever it's worth, I think Kierkegaard's generous reading of Descartes is probably the right one.

able and powerful a tool to be used so broadly and easily.

When it comes to verifying our beliefs, our situation is the reverse of a courtroom: in order to be thought rational, we must presume our beliefs false unless we can rustle up enough evidence to justify them. They are guilty until proven innocent, hanged and then sent off to the trial. Mere belief is for simpletons and the intellectually lazy.[6] It is no virtue, especially if the odds and evidence are for the moment against us (which may be the precise moment when virtue is needed).

Because the broader culture treats doubt as the apex of our intellectual experience, there are cultural incentives for those who embrace it. For young, culturally cosmopolitan evangelical Christians, the cultural rewards are all on the side of tossing out the truths we've inherited and starting again from the beginning. Trafficking in doubt draws a crowd, as anxious uncertainty strikes us as more authentic and courageous than firm conviction. It is bold to ask our questions, we think, and cowardly to retreat to the creed.

Yet I note with some irony that the genuinely revolutionary, countercultural stance is the same as ever: to say our creed with the confidence that comes from living within it and finding that it is true, good, and beautiful. In a world saturated by sarcasm and a diffident detachment from the so-called hard questions, the earnest confidence of belief confessed in the creed simply sounds different. Even when it comes from master satirist Stephen Colbert, the late-night icon of an ironic generation. He has at least three times "spontaneously" begun reciting the Nicene Creed on his show, *The Colbert Report*. His ironic non-ironic performance has enough layers to make heads spin. But each time, the audience starts with an uneasy laugher and ends with cheering. It is almost

---

6. As though there could be such a thing as "mere" belief!

as though his audience intuitively appreciates his taking a stand on something and naming it as true. In a world marked by the cool and vague emptiness of a cheapened and cynical skepticism, the sharp, bright colors of belief create a welcome and refreshing contrast.

WHEN QUESTIONING AND DOUBT ARE NOT THE SAME

Faith is not fundamentalism and doubting is not questioning. What do I mean?

The fundamentalist Christian stance has sometimes taken shape as an overreaction against a skeptical climate. In the face of intellectual and other challenges, the fundamentalist impulse is to preserve faith at any and all costs. Fundamentalism takes the form of a worry that on some level reason or science will undermine Christianity—which seems to mean ignoring them altogether. In such an environment, "faith" takes the form of holding on to a particular stance as a certainty, such that the possibility of questioning is immediately foreclosed. Such an impulse is often tied to particular views of Scripture or Genesis, but it shouldn't be. As we have seen play out in culture, the most permissive approaches to Scripture's teaching about sex sometimes lead to a rigid fundamentalism that endorses a liberal creed. The paradox is that while the fundamentalist's faith is frequently loud and comes off as very certain, it lacks the prudential confidence to wisely, but truly, face up to the questions that confront it. It is driven by a vague sense of threats that it does not know how to respond to effectively and so ends up being reduced to shouting its answers while running away.[7]

Faith is not fundamentalism—nor is doubt the same as

---

7. This sort of fundamentalism actually has very little to do with those books that are more referenced than read, *The Fundamentals*. Just for the record.

questioning. While the tendency is to react to fundamentalism by embracing doubt, I think it is important to not replace one problem with another. What we should pursue is a confident faith that questions and questions well, not the vague instability of doubt that replaces the overweening certainty of fundamentalism.

Doubt is a different phenomenon than inquiry. Notice that we even speak about the two differently. We "experience" doubt or we "have" our doubts, but we ask our questions and we question. Doubt seems to be more of a *state* or *condition*, while questioning is a pursuit. When we doubt, we hesitate over whether to welcome or accept what is before us. We waver in our stance and hold ourselves back from committing ourselves. The posture of doubt is even different from outright unbelief: it is neither the boldness of an outright rejection or the humility of belief. It is, instead, a vacillating double-mindedness that prevents us from living a fully integrated life within the world. It is to be tossed about by every wave and wind of the sea.

Our questioning may be rooted in our doubts, but it does not have to be. Conflating doubt and questioning is one of the chief confusions of our age. Reacting against perceptions of an uncritical, unreflective faith, many people have turned to the language of doubt as the best alternative. The move may be a sincere one, but it is dangerous. Failing to distinguish between doubt and questioning creates confusion and makes *commendable* to us forms of life that we may not be called to as Christians, even while there is as much room for those who doubt within the kingdom as there is for anyone else.

Faith does not close off questioning—it reforms and orients it. It is not the bunker mentality of fundamentalism, which shuts down inquiry because it is afraid. Faith seeks understanding, and the form of its seeking is the questions that it asks within the life of the practices of the church. Faith is the presupposition to questions and inquiry, the ground that we stand on as we look out and survey the world. It is not the end of our exploring but the beginning, for it engenders a love that longs to see the one whose life gives us life.

FAITH AND THE FORMATION OF OUR QUESTIONS

"My God, my God, why hast thou forsaken me?"[8] In the middle of the crucifixion, the crux of history, Jesus articulates the deepest anxiety humanity knows: whether God will be good to us in the midst of our sin and suffering. He poses a question that seems to indicate something like doubt. G. K. Chesterton once suggested that the line made Christianity "the one religion in which God seemed himself for an instant to be an atheist."[9] It is the line on which the contemporary Christian retrieval of doubt most prominently rests.

But before we embrace doubt on these grounds, we should question it a little more closely. Scripture makes room for lamentation and grief, for the bitter sorrow of deferred longing. But its exhortation and encouragement routinely move us away from doubt and toward the confidence—not the certainty but the *confidence*—of faith. For instance, the Psalms and prophets are permeated by the mournful, "How long, oh Lord?" It is a cry of sorrow and lament, a plea for God to vindicate His people and relieve their suffering. The form of the question is clearly an anxious plea; it encapsulates people's frustration at God's inactivity. But the question also depends upon and deepens the awareness that Israel is reliant upon God and His action. The question may be a form of

---

8. Matthew 27: 46 (KJV).

9. G. K. Chesterton, *Orthodoxy* (Hollywood, FL: Simon & Brown, 2012), 140.

"faith in the foxhole," but it is no less faith for it. The mournful cry of longing and frustration is simply faith in a minor key: we only pour out our hearts to those we believe will hear us and respond.

Or consider the angst that the psalmist captures: "Why are you cast down, O my soul, and why are you in turmoil against me?"[10] The psalmist's question stems from his troubled soul: "My tears have been my food day and night, while they say to me continually, 'where is your God?'" The people bothering him want evi-dence, a clear and certain answer to their skepticism about God's presence in the world. In light of this, the internal unrest of the psalmist isn't valorized or commended. It is instead the context in which exhortation and confession take place. "Hope in God, for I shall again praise Him" provides the answer to his own question, an answer that is simultaneously an exhortation. The momentary experience of doubt is expunged, driven out by the worshipful, confident hope that God will act. As a different psalmist will write when wrestling with the success of the wicked, "My flesh and my heart may fail, but God is the strength of my heart and my portion forever."[11] The answer of God's faithfulness calls into question our experience of doubt and hesitating uncertainty.

This is why moments of uncertainty in Scripture are often accompanied by calls for God to remember His covenant, to arise from His slumber and defend His people. Psalm 74 opens with a lament expressed in the form of a question: "O God, why do you cast us off forever? Why does your anger smoke against the people of your pasture?" But it closes with a supplication: "Arise, O God, defend your cause; remember how the foolish scoff at you all the day! Do not forget the clamor of your foes, the uproar of those who rise against you, which goes up continually."[12] The first

---

10. Psalm 42:5 (ESV). See also Psalm 43:5.

11. Psalm 73:26 (ESV).

12. Psalm 74:22 (ESV).

word may take the form of a question, but the psalm's character is revealed in the end: it is prayer that the psalmist partakes in, an act of faithful obedience. His frustration with God's inaction is the shape his faith takes for a moment, but that moment then resolves into hope.

While the New Testament does not provide us the rich interior vocabulary that the Psalms offers, it clearly indicates that those who follow Jesus will experience moments of uncertainty. Facing his own death, John the Baptist asks Jesus whether He was the one that they had longed for or whether they should look for someone else. Given that John's vocation was to announce the Messiah's coming, his candor is fascinating and refreshing. Despite his faithful service, his precarious position in Herod's prison prompts him to reevaluate.

John's question signals a deep affirmation that there *is* a Messiah. He has not shed that commitment or called it into question. If anything, it is his earnest confidence that God's promise of deliverance is true that moves him to inquire (again!) about the man who seems the best possible candidate.[13] We hear in John's words the anxiety of doubt, in part because ours is an anxious age. But when facing suffering or possible death, the need for confidence is all the greater. It is not the instability of doubt that moves the martyrs to take their death with a smile or that enables those like John to proclaim that one greater has arrived. John's question comes from the shadows of a prison. It is the question of a man whose life has been wrapped up in another, who has believed but has not yet seen the One he proclaimed bring about the transformation John had longed for. "Are you really He?" What looks at first glance like a wavering commitment is swept up within the painful

---

13. Notice: Jesus answers John's question. It may be a cryptic answer at first glance, but He still answers.

cross of trustful love. As Joseph Ratzinger once wrote, "We have to pose the question, 'Are you really He,' not only through honesty of thought and because of reason's responsibility, but also in accordance with the intrinsic law of love, which wants to know more and more him to whom it has given its 'Yes,' so as to be able to love him more."[14]

But the resurrection does not put an end to doubt either. The gospel accounts are very clear that the disciples are initially uncertain about how to understand the empty tomb. Luke 24:37–38 says that when Jesus appears to the disciples, some form of doubt or hesitation arises in their hearts that is not dispelled until they touch His hands and feet. They are somewhat reluctant, it seems, to go along with the idea that Jesus had been raised from the dead. But at that point, Luke writes, they "disbelieved for joy and were marveling," suggesting an overwhelming astonishment at events they could make no sense of.[15]

The gospel according to Mark also ends with a surprising note: "And [the women] went out and fled from the tomb, for trembling and astonishment had seized them, and they said nothing to anyone, for they were afraid."[16]

The uncertainty and ambiguity is haunting, but is not surprising given Mark's unique understanding of Jesus. Mark routinely hides Jesus' glory from our view in order to train our eyes to see it in surprising places. In the center of the gospel, Mark recounts a curious healing by Jesus. He puts mud on a blind man's eye and then washes it off. But the blind man is not fully healed; he can

---

14. Benedict XVI, *Introduction to Christianity* (San Francisco: Communio Books, 2004), 48–49.

15. Luke 24:41 (ESV).

16. As though troubled by the ambiguous ending, later Christians seem to have added to the manuscript.

only see "people, but they look like trees, walking."[17] So Jesus repeats the process, giving the man his full sight. Surely Jesus could have healed him the first time. So what is going on?

Immediately after that double-healing, Peter famously confesses that Jesus is the Messiah but has to be rebuked because he misunderstands what that means.[18] Peter thinks that Jesus is going to assume power through a rebellion, but Jesus' path goes through the cross—it is resurrection that Jesus brings us to, not an insurrection.[19] Like the blind man, Peter has grasped a part but not the whole. His vision is still imperfect. Only after the "second healing" of his sight by the resurrection could Peter see and understand Jesus properly.[20] Once Jesus is raised from the dead, His disciples reinterpret His whole life to see His glory in ways that they had not been able to see it before.

Mark also wants to train readers to see Jesus' life as the disciples did, which means he often leaves Jesus' glory hidden. Even in the moment of the resurrection, Mark underscores the fear and confusion of those who have not yet grasped all that the events mean. Yet while Mark leaves room for this response, he does not want us to remain confused. For in the moment of fear and uncertainty—even that prompted by the resurrection—Mark wants us to begin the gospel again and learn to see Jesus anew: "The beginning of the Gospel of Jesus Christ, the Son of God . . ."[21] The fear and uncertainty we experience even within the context of the

---

17. Mark 8:24 (ESV).

18. Mark 8:27–33 (ESV).

19. I owe this point to Brandon O'Brien.

20. The first "healing" being the transfiguration, which happens immediately following this episode. And which records the disciples as being "terrified," a stronger version of the fear that the women who came to the empty tomb knew.

21. This was in a sermon I once heard, but I don't know the name of the person who gave it. It has stayed with me for years, and I am indebted to the anonymous source (anonymous to me, but not to God). The moral of the story is, always take notes in sermons.

resurrection is the fuel we use to better understand our Savior and His world. In Mark's gospel, more than the others, we see in a mirror dimly—men walking about like trees, a man who orders those He heals to not make Him known as the Son of God.[22] Only by reading and rereading the text are we given sight. Mark's audience would have been well acquainted with fear, persecuted as it was. But by deliberately reminding us of Jesus' hidden and veiled glory, Mark gives hope to the suffering by pointing toward a God who suffered as a man as well. We learn to read the gospel differently in light of the resurrection, which transforms our faith into sight and mercifully chastens our misconceptions of the Savior.[23]

And then there is Thomas, blessed doubting Thomas, patron saint of the uncertain. He is a popular figure for understandable reasons, yet we often overlook that Jesus' expectations for Thomas were apparently different than for the rest of the disciples.[24] John makes a point to mention that Jesus "showed [the disciples] his hands and his side," presumably because He had to.[25] Thomas simply wanted what everyone else had already been given: visible and physical confirmation that Jesus had risen from the dead.[26]

Jesus' response to Thomas is indicative of the sort of emphasis the New Testament places on faith. His command is direct and straightforward: "Do not disbelieve, but believe." Nor is it limited to its context, for in the next breath Jesus suggests that those who believe without seeing Him directly (and that includes you and me) shall be "blessed." That Jesus commands belief suggests that it should not be assumed: unbelief and doubt remain possibilities,

---

22. Mark 3:12; 1:43 (ESV).

23. Which judging by some of our rhetoric today, the place where we least expect God to show up is inside the confines of the church. Which is precisely where He is waiting.

24. I owe this point to Father David Baumann.

25. John 20:20 (ESV).

26. John 20:24–25 (ESV).

even for those disciples whom Jesus has called.

But why is Thomas treated differently? Why is he chastised when no one else is, despite the fact that he only wants the physical proof the other disciples had already been given? In John's account, the apostles receive the Holy Spirit eight days before Thomas sees Jesus.[27] The disciples are in that moment endowed with the authority of Jesus to forgive sins and withhold judgment.[28] But their authority also extends to their testimony about Jesus' resurrection: Thomas is chastised for his unwillingness to accept the other disciples' authoritative witness. "Blessed are those who believe," not magically and without evidence but on the basis of the authorized witness of the apostles to the life, death, and resurrection of Jesus.[29]

If there is a lodestar for the New Testament's teaching on faith and doubt, though, it is probably James 1:6: "But let him ask in faith, with no doubting, for the one who doubts is like a wave of the sea that is driven and tossed by the wind." It is remarkable just how similar the passage is to Paul's line about not being "tossed to and fro by the waves and carried about by every wind of doctrine." The person who doubts is "double-minded" and "unstable in all his ways." James's caution against doubt is a strong one, but it fits well the exhortations to believe found throughout the entire New Testament.[30] Where the instability of doubt is present, Christ may also be there—but where Christ is, the instability of doubt may not remain, for the Christ who commands us to believe will also give to us the power to believe.

---

27. John 20:22 (ESV). This is different than Luke's account, of course, where the Holy Spirit is given at Pentecost (Acts 2:1-13). How to line up these two narratives? That is a very good question.

28. John 20:23 (ESV).

29. I owe this point to Father David Baumann.

30. I also note the following: Matthew 21:21; Jude 1:22; Matthew 14:31; Luke 24:38; Hebrews 11:1-40; Romans 14:23.

FAITH IN A MINOR KEY

The moments of doubt that we see in Scripture are taken up into the life of faith, not kept outside of it. The moments full of anxious uncertainty, such that our bones feel as though they are rotting, are transposed into another key. If we situate them within the story of the gospel, we discover that such moments are not the end. We find resolution to insecurities and instabilities not necessarily when we find answers but when we express them in prayer. We are not called to bury our doubts but to confess them. And when those near us are embroiled in doubts, it is given us to bear their crosses with them and enter into their labor alongside them. "Have mercy on those who doubt" is Jude's command, a command that can only be fulfilled when we remember the God who has had mercy on us all. [31]

Doubt is not an inevitable part of the Christian life, nor is a sign of maturity or strength—but it will always remain a possibility. Even the strong have seasons of weakness, and it is the strong who are able to acknowledge those seasons as such. The confidence of our faith in Christ is not a shrill or an easy confidence. It is not a sort of triumphalism that remains oblivious to our circumstances. Confidence has many imitators and the most pernicious might be that which always speaks with the right answer. "In quietness and in trust shall be your strength," Isaiah writes. [32] We have this confidence only when we soberly and truthfully confess the frailty of our belief and praise the faithfulness of God to His people despite the appearances. When the man cries out, "I believe; Help my unbelief!" a faith that will grow into confidence is formed in Him.

But as long as we live in a fallen world, our faith *must* include

31. Jude 1:22 (ESV).
32. Isaiah 30:15 (ESV).

tears and sorrow for evils and injustices. Lamentation keeps doubt at bay. The absence of genuine, sorrowful mourning in our worship services and communities is more to blame for the rise of doubt and instability among younger Christians than any French philosopher ever could be.[33] The absence of lamentation is a failure to preach the whole counsel of God—which includes an entire book devoted to *Lamentations*. And it leaves a gap where unhealthy expressions of uncertainty take root and flourish. When suffering and evil come upon us, if we have not been taught to respond well, then we are all but assured of responding badly.

The freedom to bring our laments before God and utter our complaints in the presence of the Most High is one of the best "answers" we have to our experiences of anger, frustration, and doubt. In C. S. Lewis's most profound novel, *Till We Have Faces*, the queen raises her grievances against the gods for their (allegedly) unjust treatment. As she reads, she slowly becomes aware that her meticulously prepared manuscript has been reduced to a single paragraph—a paragraph that she is simply repeating. For once they are uttered in the presence of the Almighty, our complaints turn out to be much less substantial than they initially seemed. The process ends for the queen when a god speaks: "Enough. Are you answered?" Her only response can be yes, for in his presence the lament and the satisfaction are one and the same.[34]

In the same way, Jesus' cry on the cross seems from one vantage point to be a moment of anguish. "My God, my God, why have you forsaken me?" It is a heart-wrenching moment, a cry of agony. But from the vantage point of the resurrection, the cry of despair is transposed into a pregnant cry of triumph, a triumph

---

33. We give French philosophers too much credit and therefore too much blame.
34. C. S. Lewis, *Till We Have Faces: A Myth Retold* (New York: Harcourt, Brace, 1957).

that cost no less than everything and that has a tragedy at its center. In the same vein, the psalmist's mournful "How long?" becomes John's "*Maranatha!*" "Come quickly, Lord Jesus!" The hopeful confidence of faith goes deeper than words can reach: as noted above, the resurrection is so strong and overwhelming that "disbelief for joy" becomes an apt expression for our response to it. This fundamental transposition of joy has been felt in our churches only as often as our laments, which is why the word "joy" has become so cheapened and neutered. For it is a joy whose power comes to us through the sorrow of the cross and our encounter with it. But here, at the center of belief and unbelief, the cry of Jesus reminds us that the momentary experience of abandonment cannot be trusted; it must be called into question.

The cry of lament becomes the cry of victory. Jesus is quoting Psalm 22, only He wants us to go beyond that line of the psalm. The Jewish people didn't simply quote a verse: they quoted a verse that brought the entire passage to mind for hearers.[35] Psalm 22 begins with a question about God's absence, but like most laments in the Psalms, it moves toward an affirmation of God's faithfulness: "For he has not despised or abhorred the affliction of the afflicted, and *he has not hidden his face from him*, but has heard, when he cried to him."[36] The expression of doubt is the context for the glorious affirmation of God's unrelenting faithfulness. The poem closes with the cry that future generations shall proclaim that the "Lord has done it," that He has rescued His beloved from his adversaries. Despite the appearances, when we look backward from the

---

35. Peter Rollins notes that Jesus says this in Aramaic, His native tongue, rather than the language of the Old Testament. I suspect that has more to do with the depths to which Jesus integrated the Word into Himself, rather than an indication that He is leaving behind what was the standard Jewish practice of reading. See Peter Rollins, *Insurrection: To Believe Is Human, to Doubt, Divine* (London: Hodder & Stoughton, 2011), 25.

36. Emphasis mine.

resurrection upon the cross, we see that all the promises of God are ever and always *yes* and *amen* to the glory of God—and that the *yes* and *amen* are brought about by a God who destroys every evil and offers a joy that overwhelms every sorrow.

FAITHFUL QUESTIONING AND THE LAW OF LOVE

The attempt to rescue doubt to deepen the Christian life is a correction against our culture's anemic understanding of faith and the hostility toward questioning it produces. But sometimes remedies prove worse than the disease. And a superficial understanding of faith has led to an equally reductionistic notion of doubt. The Bible knows much of lamentation and brokenness, of pleading for Christ's return, and of the prayer for strength and for a more confident belief. It knows of those who have proclaimed that the anchor held, even while it was sorely tested. But that is the paradox of faith: the surer our commitment to the power of God's promises, the louder our lament will be as we wait to see those promises fulfilled. The more unwavering our affirmation of God's goodness, the more resolved will be our pursuit of justice. The more we trust in His Word, the more we will question ourselves.

The way forward is the way of faith, a faith that does not deny questioning but orients questions toward understanding and grounds them in love. For faith is the pretext for questioning well, the atmosphere that sustains patient, longing inquiry. "Faith comes by hearing,"[37] Paul tells us: it is the welcoming into ourselves of something that we have not predetermined. It is that which comes to us that engenders our faith, not that which we discover or possess. Faith precedes our searching and exploring and thus makes it possible.

---

37. Romans 10:17 NKJV.

The faith the Word creates is the fullness of a life. In Romans 4 Paul treats Abraham as the paradigmatic representative of faithful obedience, as evidenced by his "hope against hope" that God would be faithful to His promise. "He did not waver in unbelief," Paul suggests but "grew strong in faith" through giving glory to God. Yet the strength of Abraham's faith does not stem from denial or dismissiveness. His reliance on the promise frees him to consider and explore the implausible circumstances in which the word was given. Paul notes that Abraham "contemplated his own body," which was "now as good as dead" and the "deadness of Sarah's womb." God's work of faith that makes us *new creations* happens in the confrontation with death and our creaturely limitations.[38]

Faith in the promises of God takes root in our hearts amidst the barrenness of the world and the death present within our own bodies. We trust and explore, trust and seek understanding. We trust and lament, trust and return to the promises of God with the "hope against hope" that He will not disappoint. We trust and turn from sin, trust and confront the vanity of the world and the emptiness that is passing away. We see the injustice and suffering and return to Calvary. The confidence of our faith must be rooted in the cross, for through His death Christ is faithful to His promises and ushers in the newness of life.

Faith opens up a world that is not of our own making, a world that we are given to search out and enjoy. While the first movement of faith is prayer and the final is worship, between them lie the questioning and exploring. The life of faith liberates our questioning from the anxious burden of justifying ourselves, for when we live within the domain of the cross, we rejoice in Christ's justification of us. Jesus' triumphal cry of dereliction is a question asked

---

38. All the translations in this paragraph are taken from the NASB.

once, for all. And once answered in the resurrection, the finality of it sets those who are in Christ free to pursue their inquiries with the knowing confidence that Jesus shall direct and redirect their exploratory steps as He deems fit.

For like any place, this land that we are given in faith also has limits and boundaries that give it a unique and distinctive character. Our trust in the Scriptures does not close off our questioning, but it does reorder it. Some paths that were once before us no longer become relevant possibilities for inquiry in the same way. We cannot, for instance, "suspend judgment" on whether Christianity is true as though we are standing beyond and outside of it and rendering a verdict in the court of law. As Austin Farrer put it, "You might as well recommend to a husband the rational duty of suspending judgment about his wife's fidelity until he has tested it by a sufficient number of ingenious traps and artificial maneuvers."[39] If our faith makes us who we are, then all our questioning happens within the borders of faith.[40]

Questions that we pursue within the life of faith have a unique tenor. The questioning of faith is a confident questioning, a questioning that knows the answer we seek is already known by God and will be revealed to us when we are ready. We may wonder whether God exists or if He is good, but such momentary irruptions are relativized and their significance deflated. We can have our anxieties, say them to God, and then go about our business. And we can confidently take up the question of whether God exists by thinking through the world as though He didn't and seeing where it all gets us. That sort of imaginative exploration is safe in the context of faith because we are kept within the hand of God. Nor does it mean the arguments we come up with in that process

---

39. Austin Farrer, *A Faith of Our Own* (Cleveland: World Pub., 1960), 96.

40. Even, I would note, the imaginative exploration of other conceptions of the topography.

are any less reasonable because we have not let go of our commitment to Christianity. The reasonability of an argument does not hinge upon the commitments of the person making it but upon the argument itself. If anything, imaginative exploration should help us find new and more interesting ways of putting things. For we will start to see reasons everywhere for what we know to be true, and we can listen and deliberate patiently and with a generous confidence among those who disagree. If we are seeking understanding, as faith necessarily does, then we have nothing to fear. But we do not weigh Christianity in the balances. We instead question differently, and in some cases ask different questions, out of our commitment to the revelation of God in Jesus Christ.

For while the creed establishes the topography of the land we inherit, it does not necessarily exhaustively explain it or immediately bring us to see it. Instead, faith necessarily takes the shape of inquiry and pursues its proper end: the joyful good of loving understanding, an understanding that reciprocally enhances and deepens our love.

4

What Counts as
Satisfaction?

What shall I say? Where's satisfaction?—IAGO [1]

My first two years after college, I spent hundreds of hours leading high school students in discussions as part of a supplemental education program for homeschoolers.[2] The conversations varied widely, as the reading list took us everywhere from the role of women in society to the nature of the American political founding. Few subjects went unexplored and while I did my best to keep the discussions away from controversy, we somehow kept finding our way there. I have no idea how it happened.

Most of my students were new to the loosely structured intellectual environment that the conversations created. And many of them were quickly frustrated. I would open class with a question about their reading and they would set about answering it. Or try

---

1. William Shakespeare, *Othello* (Norman Sanders, ed. Cambridge; New York: Cambridge University Press, 1984), Act 3, Scene 3.
2. Yes, those exist. And they are awesome. And so are, by the way, homeschoolers.

n they were still getting the hang of things, they
out in circles, growing increasingly irritated at
lack of "progress." My students trusted me, but then
they didn't have much of a choice. Because while I was happy to
explain my methods, I fiercely refused to give them any answers.

They frequently complained about my reluctance to tell them
what to think—or even what I thought—but I wasn't particularly
concerned by their plight. In my worst moments, their groans
were even a source of mischievous amusement. I wanted them to
be more aware of what they didn't know than what they did. I was
more concerned to hear them ask a question well than see them
rush over the question for a hurried, trivial answer. Answers to
the questions we care most deeply about often seem impossibly
elusive and to communicate otherwise to my students by playing
the guru would do them a gross disservice. From the first moment
I started teaching, I treated my students as those who needed to
think and inquire like adults.

Besides, having the proverbial lightbulb go off is such a pre-
cious experience that I didn't want to shortchange anyone from
seeing or experiencing it. High school students are fun because
they don't have the sober, pretentious self-consciousness that we
sometimes adopt as we grow older. So when moments of insight finally arrive, they often don't hold back. When they catch a glimpse
of a meaningful answer, you can see it on their faces: the impulse
to speak wells up within them until it spills over into words. The
torrent that is released is rarely as coherent and compelling as it
seemed in their heads, but that doesn't matter much—and students
get better at articulating themselves with practice. The sheer joy
that prompts them to shout their metaphorical "Eureka!" is a foreign or forgotten experience to many of us, but when it takes hold
it is a true wonder.

Are Answers the Answer?

There's a hilarious scene in that beacon of the American comedic tradition, *Parks and Recreation*, in which the incompetent, mentally childlike millionaire Bobby Newport debates the show's hero, Leslie Knope, for a spot on the city council. In his closing statement, Newport makes his appeal with a sense of candor that would be refreshing from a politician: "How do we fix this town? I have no idea. You tell me. That's what I'm counting on. You telling me. I will ask lots of questions. You give me answers. Questions are great, but answers are better. And answers phrased as questions—is how you play Jeopardy."[3]

Serious comedy. Clearly.[4] But Newport nails precisely how we tend to approach learning: Questions are great, but answers really *are* better.

Look at our educational system. For the most part, teachers reward students for the answers they give rather than the questions they ask. By the time my students arrived in high school, they were proficient in the art of providing ready-made responses to prefabricated questions.[5] Teacher asks question, students answer; rinse and repeat. That approach never cost students anything, except maybe a few hours of cramming (if that). And it certainly didn't teach them to come up with questions themselves—what some people call "thinking."

Answers may sometimes be "better," but they are not enough. I remember one class in which a particularly sharp student spoke up after I asked my opening question. What followed was every discussion leader's worst nightmare: my masterfully crafted lead-in and my plans for the class were dispensed with by the stu-

---

3. Amy Poehler, *Parks and Recreation*, "The Debate" (Los Angeles: Deedle-Dee Productions, April 26, 2010).

4. Fisticuffs for those who disagree.

5. And those were *homeschoolers*, who are supposed to be "countercultural."

dent's equally masterful, impressively thorough, true response.[6] I was in awe, frankly, and uncertain about how to respond. So after a deliberate pause, I remarked that it was an interesting point and quickly asked the rest of the class what they thought. Over the course of the discussion, the young lady who had initially responded made several less impressive arguments that betrayed a lack of clarity and understanding about her own "right answer." While the class eventually came around to where she had begun, she moved in a different direction: her initial clarity became a sort of confusion as she tried to work out the arguments for it. By the end, she returned to where she started too—but with more and more clear reasons why and how we should all adopt her position.

I wasn't being mischievous or even trying to make a point. But neither she nor the class came around to the "same" place at all, even though the sentence that answered the question at the beginning and the end used the exact same words. Through the questioning and reason-giving that went on, everyone's understanding of the issue was sharpened. When we set out, the student could give the right answer but not the reasons for it—or at least not very well. Others read the right parts of the text but didn't grasp its meaning. Some came to a reasonable interpretation but didn't understand its implications. Which is to say, the class may have begun with a student being correct. And they ended there, too. But in between there was growth and development, deepening and refining, such that the beginning and the end seemed different even though they were the same.

---

6. One moral of this story is that perhaps my preparations were not all that I remember them to be.

SEEK UNDERSTANDING

Facts are cheap. We have access to nearly every piece of data we could possibly want through the Internet. The value of information as a raw material has dropped precipitously, with the exception of some time-sensitive subjects, like finance and the news, where speed still commands a price. But for most of us, the only cost of accessing information is the constant and inescapable presence of advertising.

What we need is the ability to bring those facts together into a compelling narrative. The synthetic act of understanding, of seeing how pieces of information work together and make a meaningful whole, is a skill that no amount of Googling can ever teach us. Understanding is the currency of our increasingly fragmented world; demand for the ability to gain and convey understanding has skyrocketed as the amount of accessible information has increased.

Understanding requires intimacy with a subject. It is the fruit of a sympathetic attentiveness, a willingness to consider carefully what is before us with the peculiar desire to learn more about it—rather than (necessarily) determine whether what we think about it is true. Understanding also comes in degrees—one person may understand astrophysics more than another, but both people would certainly understand more than I do. And sometimes the fullness of understanding requires living inside a subject and seeing it from within. We might understand how baseball works on the surface: three strikes makes an out, three outs in an inning, and base runners advance a base on a balk. But the game's texture and dynamics often remain opaque to us who have never had firsthand familiarity with the players and clubhouse.[7] We do not see how

---

7. Unless they consume lots and lots of literature about these things. While such knowledge would be secondhand, the imaginative grasp might be able to reach a point where it would be virtually equivalent to firsthand knowledge. At least I think. How this works is, admittedly, an open question to me.

the game *really* works, how all the moving parts work together, and how the "intangibles" play out on the field.

Searching for information on the Internet is easy; pursuing understanding is hard. The former meets a felt need quickly and without effort. But the latter enables us to live well and flows from our living well. Google may solve a gap in our information, but the question of how we shall live, of what sort of friends we should seek, whether we should give our money to a charity in Africa or to the homeless man on the street—those are questions that will seize our attention when we place ourselves in environments where they arise. If we never encounter poverty, we may struggle to seriously wrestle with how we should use our resources. To know how we must respond, we must understand ourselves and the world, see how they work, and discern the peculiar shape of life to which we have been called. All our reading or browsing is insufficient to give us wisdom without reading and questioning ourselves along with it.

Compared to the easy answers, the long, tumultuous, and frequently painful work of seeking understanding seems really hard and generally useless. I understand why my students kicked against my methods and occasionally complained that I was being "mean." Their habits of mind have been trained in a very different direction, as have all of ours. But questioning well means more than "finding an answer" so that we can simply get on with our lives. Those who inquire well must move from answers to understanding, from the instant gratification of our need for comfort and security toward the deepened desire for the enduring good of wisdom.

LIVING INTO THE ANSWERS

In the lovable and surprisingly mature comic strip *Peanuts*, Lucy would occasionally set up a lemonade stand—as any child might. Only Lucy didn't sell lemonade: she sold answers and advice for the pretty penny of five cents. Her most regular customer, the endearingly depressed Charlie Brown, appeared on September 22 of 1963 and asked her what someone should do when he doesn't fit in and life seems to be passing him by. Lucy led Charlie Brown to the top of a hill and engaged him in a mini-Socratic dialogue:

> See the horizon over there? See how big this world is? See how much room there is for everybody? Have you ever seen any other worlds? *No.* As far as you know, this is the only world there is, right? *Right.* There are no other worlds for you to live in . . . right? *Right.* You were born to live in this world . . . right? *Right.*

The dialogue concludes with Lucy at her most forceful: "WELL, LIVE IN IT THEN!" she shouts while Charlie flips backward. It's an amusing and powerful response. Probably worth more than the five cents Lucy takes for her services.[8]

Like Charlie Brown, we all want answers to our deepest questions. Answers provide us with a sense of stability. The more understanding we have, the more at home in the world we feel. When we are unsure about our own commitments and we waver between them, our lives can seem off-kilter. Reflective individuals will often feel gaps where others do not, which sometimes allows questioning and doubts to get in the way of the simplicity of action. We need, or so we think, answers and clarity before we feel

---

8. Charles Schulz, *Peanuts*, September 22, 1963. http://www.gocomics.com/peanuts/1963/09/22.

like we can "live in it, then."

I was reminded of this danger during a conversation with a senior British fellow, who had converted to Christianity late in life but was brimming with wisdom. "Sometimes," he told me, "I think we ought to wake up in the morning and say 'Lord, have mercy,' and then *get on with it.*" Cultivating a reliance on the providence of God to transform us frees us from obsessive self-reflection that can undermine our confidence in Christ's sometimes slow, sometimes imperceptible sanctifying work. We should not be surprised by moments of doubt or uncertainty. But the paradox is that the more we grasp our own frailty and the strength of God's mercy, the more we can simply "get on with it" and about our day. The Christian life is not constituted by having answers to all our deepest questions but by a life of trustful repose in the gracious sovereignty of God. We live the questions, but as Rainer Maria Rilke put it in the *other* part of the quote, we may "gradually and imperceptibly live [our] way into the answer."[9]

Still, the thorny question of how we shall live sits beneath many of our anxieties and our frustrations. While our lives often conform to the environments in which we place ourselves, when we do dig up our presuppositions and our unreflective commitments and enter into the examined life, the way forward can prove difficult to find. When we are confronted with problems we cannot solve or events our understanding cannot make sense of, we explore and search out to find understanding.

That pursuit can often feel like wandering about without quite knowing where we are going, which is—if nothing else is—a foreign sensation to most of us. Our contemporary reliance on smart phones and maps means we no longer know the frustrations of getting lost. The anxieties and worries it evokes can be quite

---

9. Rilke, *Letters*, 46.

taxing. We wander about, half-recognizing objects in our hope we've found where we are while being weighed down with the disappointment of getting it wrong. We take off in one direction only to arrive back where we started. Our progress is halting and often doesn't feel like we're going anywhere at all. But when we arrive—the relief and comfort arrival provides is euphoric.

It's no wonder, then, that we are willing to shell out significant amounts of money to find the answers we feel we need to live well. Many of us (appropriately) have yielded the task of questioning ourselves to the professionalized realm of the counselor or therapist's office. We pay a good deal more than Lucy's fee. But the guide through the wilderness and the questions that they ask us often turn out to be more than worth it.

Others go for the low-cost solution, outsourcing their questions to the sprawling self-help industry. We set up gurus and follow them, buying their ready-made solutions to life's deepest problems. It's a quick fix we're after, a comforting and prompt response to questions that deserve lifetimes of exploration. Honestly, the temptation makes some sense. It's easy to rail against the "therapeutic" without appreciating the sort of comfort neat and tidy affirmations actually provide. Such answers may not ultimately satisfy, but they are insufficient for being distortions and approximations of the truth—rather than being totally opposed to it.

Besides, we ought not be among those casting the first stones, should we? As Christians, we want our pastors to dispense answers the way columnists pass out advice: by giving us just enough instruction so we know what to do but not so much that we have to think. We have our own Christian "guidance" industry, with its gurus and its "tribes" and its ready-to-order fixes. The advice may be better than that from other books, and even quite biblical. But they are written and packaged to satisfy the "consumer's" immediate felt needs rather than remind him of his true needs and draw him deeper into them.

Of course, knowing what to do isn't bad. It's important to know how to live—and important to seek sound advice. My concern is that our answer-dispensing industrial complex is short-circuiting the work of empowering people and communities to patiently linger over the questions so that their growth into understanding is set within their sorrows and joys together as the church. Providing the answers from the pulpit or even in the small group cannot equip us to become mature thinkers and followers on our own. If we want people to think adult thoughts, then we should stop catering to their felt needs for quick answers.

We Christians should not be so answers oriented that we render ourselves incapable of coming up with the questions ourselves.[10] We might think it a miracle that anyone learned about the Bible before we had study guides, given our total dependence upon them. What questions could the early Christians have possibly asked without the prompts we now have? And how did readers ever learn from books without prepackaged questions at the end of each chapter? If we are going to move beyond being a community that simply regurgitates "easy answers," then we must also be willing to put an end to spoon-feeding the questions.

The apologetics community, which is a corner of Christianity that has placed a very high value on having answers, has remained busy composing arguments for the faith while equipping loyal followers to do the same. They've done enormous good and have instilled countless Christians with a good deal of healthy confidence. And as Austin Farrer once pointed out, "what no one

---

10. Or maybe the problem is that we don't write books that *breed* questions in readers. That is a problem as well.

shows the ability to defend is quickly abandoned."[11] The task of countering objections to Christianity is an ancient vocation and we ought not to put an end to it now.

But the work of providing reasons for Christianity has teetered on overcompensating for the anti-intellectual strains in American Christianity and the rise of a noisy atheist opposition. The first and most important aim of the Christian intellect is not to defend the answers we affirm or to critique those who disagree with us but to understand in its fullness the revelation we have been given.[12] Confidence flows from understanding, and understanding is the intellectual fruit of love. Confidence is a by-product: it is not an end in itself. Answers and arguments are not primarily tools to improve our witness to the lost or to increase our confidence in the truthfulness of Christianity. They are instead moments in our formation as obedient and loving disciples, given to us to help us more faithfully walk in the footsteps of Jesus and love Him more deeply. Such a disposition toward answers and arguments allows us to speak confidently and authoritatively while still maintaining a humble awareness of the limits of our own knowledge.

What's more, the focus on answers and arguments in apologetics sometimes has made us inattentive to the questions being asked. There are times and places to have arguments that are won or lost (namely, in formal settings when those are the rules). But with our neighbors, conversations are more fun and instructive when they take the form of mutual reason-giving and explaining. When the impulse to defend takes hold, we tend to short-circuit the work of understanding. Which, ironically, makes it harder to

---

11. Jocelyn Gibb and Owen Barfield, *Light on C. S. Lewis* (New York: Harcourt, Brace & World, 1966), 26.

12. Paul's prayer for the Philippians is that their love would abound "more and more, with knowledge and all discernment" (Philippians 1:9 ESV). I take it that this theme pervades his writings.

engage in spirited, lively, and open discussion with those who think about the world very differently than we do. Our instinctive disposition will be to reach into the argumentative bag of tricks rather than to listen attentively and dialogue in love. [13]

The apologetics community has tended to be the first step in many people's experience of the life of the Christian mind in part because it has (helpfully) stepped in to critical gaps in the church's formation. Many young people's experience of the church was that it was not a place of rigorous, intellectual formation but of fun and games. But we can only grow in understanding of that which we have initially grasped in outline. Which is to say, we cannot understand how an engine works if we do not already know that there is a car and it has an engine. Those two pieces of information are the necessary precursors for understanding. If we are not given answers and reasons when we are young, then we will not learn to aim our intellectual loves toward understanding. And when we first encounter challenges, we will either respond with a reactionary defensiveness or reject our answers altogether.

In that sense, the recovery of the practice of catechesis is one of the most hopeful signs for Christians interested in cultivating their ability to question and live into the answers. Christians throughout history have used catechisms to train those new to the faith in the fundamentals. Answers were often memorized, with the goal that they would be internalized so that the catechumen could have a lively dialogue with the teacher. As Christians recover the practice of catechesis, our questions will become more sophisticated because we will have a more robust framework through which to look at the world. The apologetics movement, in fact, could think of its own work through this lens. Answers

---

13. Have I done this perfectly? Of course not! My first instinct is *still* to defend answers, rather than inquire. But there are signs of hope more broadly: check out Wheatstone Academy, for instance.

and particular reasons almost never persuade people. But internalizing them lays a helpful foundation that allows for the more lively and productive back-and-forth of dialoguing together.

The Answers beneath Our Questions

It's tempting for those who first pick up questions to think that it is answers that are the problem and that we should dispense with the possibility of finding them altogether. It's an old temptation, one that William Blake had no kind words for in his epic poem *Milton*. Near the end of the poem, when Milton arrives from heaven, Blake writes that he comes:

> To cast off the idiot Questioner, who is always questioning
> But never capable of answering, who sits with a sly grin
> Silent plotting when to question, like a thief in a cave;
> Who publishes doubt and calls it knowledge. [14]

Strong words, to be sure. But the sort of pervasive skepticism that Blake denounces is not merely wearisome. It turns out to be impossible.

I am constantly losing my keys. It's a bit of a problem for me, as each time it happens I get frustrated with myself that I've done it again. The paradox of the lost keys is a funny one: if I knew where the keys were, I wouldn't have to search for them. But because I don't know where they are, I don't know where to look. The feeling is aggravating, especially when the cause is urgent: I know my keys are out there, somewhere, but because I don't know where, I end up feeling stuck. [15]

What do we do in such moments? Generally we piece together

---

14. William Blake and David V. Erdman, *The Complete Poetry and Prose of William Blake*, ed. by Harold Bloom (Berkeley: Univ. of Calif. Press, 1982), 142.

15. This is a paradox first articulated by Plato in his *Meno*, though he didn't use the example of searching for keys.

what we can remember and what we know. We retrace our steps. We eliminate possibilities. We sit back and wait, in hopes that we will be struck with an insight. As we search, we attend to the world differently than we do when we are not looking. We look beneath the couch cushions and go through our desk drawers with a care we do not have otherwise. We fill out our picture of the relevant parts of our lives to see whether the negative space before us might become filled in and we might reach the end of our exploring.

What we know aids us in our search, in other words, and as we come to know more, we can search better. And we even know something about the "unknown." For instance, we know *that* something is unknown to us (namely, the location of our keys). And the knowledge we gain as we search helps us recognize the right answer when we finally stumble over it. When I come upon my keys, I often have the sensation of relief not only at finding my keys but of seeing how I lost them in the first place.

My point here is simple: searching and questioning require presuppositions. We cannot explore the shape of the unknown except by sharpening our sense of what we do know and refining the commitments that we have. A question sends us out into the world on an expedition, but we still come from somewhere and have some conception of what we are looking for. Our questions come from within a framework, which shapes the answers that we seek. In the case of the keys, the joint knowledge that I do have keys and that it is important for me to find them motivate my search. There's something at stake for me in finding them, such that I can't really rest content until I've remembered where they are or replaced them.

For the better part of a decade, I have wrestled with what role our human bodies play in our knowledge of God and our love for one another. My questions were motivated by a sense of frustration at a perceived gap in my understanding: I knew bodies mattered, but I did not know how or why. And I knew that I had little teaching about bodies when I was growing up. I also knew that I had committed myself to believing in a God who took on a physical body in the person of Jesus, a commitment that not only motivated my questioning but also directed it. The combination of those commitments has generated a massive amount of energy in me to seek understanding of that area of our lives and to reform my own life in light of that understanding.

One of the side effects of the notion that questioning comes out of our commitments is that not everyone will find our questions equally interesting or important, as they do not share our beliefs. Whether hell exists and whether anyone is in it are important questions to us Christians. But they have a good deal less purchase outside our community as *questions*. The concepts of hell and its inhabitants may come up as objections, as reasons not to be a Christian. Or they may be raised and explored by those attempting to understand Christian teaching, on grounds that they are trying to determine whether to enter the faith or not.

But those within the Christian faith approach the question from the stance of having made (and remade and remade!) a confession of sin and of having made a profession that reality's shape can only be known through faith in the person of Jesus, the judgment of the cross, and the triumph of the resurrection. Such a stance changes what we find plausible as an account of reality and shifts the terrain so that we may find it acceptable to remain Christians without fully working out exactly how hell works or who is in it. What others might consider a reason to not be a Christian, in other words, given their presuppositions, Christians might only see as a difficulty that we are patiently exploring and working out. We see in that mirror dimly, after all.

What's more, the limited and partial understanding that we come to through our lives actually shuts off some of the possible paths before us. The moment I got married, the question of whether I was the marrying type was answered definitively and finally. I am not free to "weigh the evidence" about divorce as though it were a fifty-fifty proposition for me. I do not wake up every morning and evaluate things anew and wonder whether I will remain married that day. My commitment to my wife predetermines the questions I am free to pursue.

Of course, I still inquire within and about my marriage. But my questions have changed. Now that I stand within the relationship and see things from the inside, my questions are aimed at living well as a husband. We find ourselves together: How shall we make the best of it? Have I done all that I can to create an environment of warmth and trust? What is it with women and wicker baskets? How have we ended up *here*, so busy with our lives with what seems like so little time to talk? Why do all the joys seem so much deeper now, so much more enduring—even though they're mixed up with moments of pain and distance?

The way we form our lives will move some questions to the margins and bring others to the center. But there can be no questions if there are no commitments. For faith is the necessary framework out of which our search for understanding is pursued.

REMEMBERING THE QUESTION OF JESUS

"Jesus is the answer." Yes, but what that means depends entirely on the question. When Christian teenagers enter the university, the "Sunday school answers" that once served them well all of a sudden start to seem trite and simplistic. For some, their introduction into a critical, reflective posture toward the answers they learned in Sunday school devolves into dismissing them altogether. Others transform their faith from cliché into cliché, as they adopt trendier truisms to replace the old ones.

But "Jesus is the answer" doesn't have to be a cop-out or cliché. For some, the realization comes at the end of a lot of hardnosed inquiry into life's most difficult questions. What sort of God could possibly allow suffering?[16] How can we remake a broken and sinful world?[17] And there are others. The longer we spend working through those questions, the more prepared we will be to hear the transformative power of the gospel when we are confronted by it. In that moment, "Jesus is the answer" becomes a reverential, joyfully exuberant affirmation of the glorious reality of God's love. In that moment, all our longing is transformed into worship.

But there are some questions we pursue that will necessarily lead to frustration because only Jesus can sufficiently answer them. Consider early Christianity's relationship with Plato, who pursued questions as well as anyone else. You might say Plato grasped some of the fundamental questions: How does an individual relate to community? How do we begin on our journey into understanding? What would we do if we saw a perfectly just man? How shall we overcome the shadow of death, the mortality of the body? While Plato wrestled long and hard with the questions, he did not have the answers. Those only came, the early Christians argued, in the person of Jesus.

Jesus is primarily the answer to His own questions, though. Plato's presuppositions are not those of the Old Testament. The Bible has its own set of inquiries, which as we walk with Jesus we learn to pose. What does it mean that Jesus is the Messiah? How will God be faithful to His people? What is the nature of Christ's

---

16. Answer: a God willing to subject Himself to it.

17. Answer: We can't. For all that will live must also die, but God.

union with the Father? What is the relationship between Christ's two natures? And maybe most importantly, how should we understand Jesus' sacrificial death? While we are able to grasp some of its meaning without the Old Testament, we can only understand the atonement correctly within the context in which it was given: it makes no sense to speak of Jesus as the "Lamb of God" without understanding the rituals of sacrifice and absolution for Israel's transgressions in the Torah. [18]

Which is to say, Jesus is the answer; but the life of Jesus teaches us questions of its own. The witness of the gospel turned Platonism on its head by offering a solution to Plato's problems that Plato himself could never have imagined: the incarnation. But that answer went so deep into the framework that Platonism couldn't last. The words may have stayed the same, but the categories were co-opted and redefined. The incarnation inaugurated a new paradigm, opening up new avenues of inquiry. The early Christians did not quit thinking once they believed in Jesus. But their newfound faith changed their questions, reinvigorating an intellectual world that had otherwise come to exhaustion. [19] In attempting to understand the salvation they received, Christians set about exploring who Jesus was. And that has proved a question the depths of which we still have not fully explored.

To speak of Jesus as an "answer," though, does not encapsulate the sort of satisfaction that we experience when we encounter Him. There are some questions for which a name, a sentence, or even a cluster of ideas would be wholly unsatisfactory if set forth as an "answer." Why should I get up in the morning and

---

18. Other fun questions: Why is salvation described as "new creation"? Why does Jesus call Himself the "Son of Man"? And certainly there are others.

19. This is a point taken from Charles Norris Cochrane, *Christianity and Classical Culture: A Study of Thought and Action from Augustus to Augustine* (Indianapolis: Liberty Fund, 2003).

go off to work? We might lay down a pro/con list in order to persuade ourselves. But a list of benefits and drawbacks stacked up against each other is a reductionistic way of understanding the question before us and the sort of satisfaction that we desire in seeing an answer. It may be, for instance, that one of the goods outweighs *any* potential drawback—and that what in a given moment seem to be drawbacks are actually precisely those things that God wishes to "use for good" in our lives. Seeing the point of our work requires discerning its place in the whole of our lives, stretching our minds backward toward our birth and forward toward and beyond death to make sense of the particular moment. It is the psalmist's imaginative awareness of the brevity of his life in Psalm 90 that prompts him to turn toward God to see the work of his hands established and confirmed. The answer to the question of the meaning of our work goes well beyond a sentence: it can only be found in the life we share with the triune God.

And sometimes, the story we receive in answer to our question subverts the question altogether. The famous parable of the Good Samaritan is perhaps the best example.[20] A lawyer asks Jesus, "What shall I do to inherit eternal life?" Jesus responds by questioning what the lawyer finds in the Torah. The lawyer answers well, summarizing the law with the double command to love God and our neighbor. Yet he is not quite satisfied. He puts a further question to Jesus: "And who is my neighbor?" Jesus' response is the parable, which replaces the man's question with a more appropriate one: "Which of these three . . . *proved to be a neighbor* to the man who fell among the robbers?" The lawyer's original inquiry about his salvation was the right one. But as Jesus' story reveals, the appropriate question is not who around us counts as deserving of our love; the appropriate question is

---

20. Luke 10:25–37 (ESV).

whether we will be ready to dispense mercy to any who need it.

In a sense, Jesus is "the answer" to our fundamental questions. However, His gift to us is more than even a story; it is life itself and life abundantly. We enfold the gospel story into our lives, which lends that life its distinctive character and shape. As we hear and retell the good news, it becomes for us a story that we also live.[21] The invitation to follow this Savior is not separate from His pronouncement of the message: it is embedded within the story itself and makes a claim on our attention and our lives. And when we give ourselves to the One whose life we see on display, the faith makes us new and engenders a love that moves us to understand all we have been given. The story of Jesus is a truthful answer. But it is a truth that is understood from within, as we walk in the footsteps of the One who also declares Himself the way.

---

21. "If any man would come after me, let him deny himself . . ." (Matthew 16:24; Mark 8:34; Luke 9:23 ESV).

5

The World and
Our Questions of It

*Is the sky the limit? Will there be green thoughts
in the future?* —PADGETT POWELL[1]

"How should the fact that the author of the fourth gospel describes himself as 'the disciple whom Jesus loved' determine our understanding of it?"

And with that, I opened six hours of examining the gospel according to John with my high school students. As starter questions go, mine had problems. The question is simultaneously too narrow and too complex, and it presupposes a lot of knowledge about John's account. Those weaknesses made it a rough start out of the gates, but things improved once we were well under way.

The question's main strength is that it is unusual. It's not the sort of question that a reader picking up the gospel for the first time would likely ask. And maybe not the fifteenth time, either, which is closer to the situation I was facing. Most of my students

---

1. Padgett Powell, *The Interrogative Mood: A Novel?* (New York: Ecco, 2009).

had been raised in church and knew the story inside and out (or thought they did). But when I posed my question, they responded with a collective, "Huh!?" They hadn't the foggiest idea where to start. But the direction we eventually found was quite fruitful, leading to lots of interesting thoughts about the relationship between love and testimony—even if we admittedly were crawling through a backdoor into the text rather than approaching it head-on.[2]

It's hard to have interesting and meaningful conversations about the Bible with Christians. *Really* hard.[3] Biblical literacy isn't a strong point of American culture, but most active small group participants have a healthy familiarity with the text. Rather than make for more interesting discussions, though, our proximity to Scripture often has the reverse effect. People who know the "right answers" often think they are sufficient. Or people feel like they *should* have the right answers, making them reluctant to speak up.[4]

My goal when teaching was twofold: I wanted to find a question that my students didn't think they already knew the answer to and I wanted to make the familiar seem strange. What they had seen straight, I wanted them to see crooked. What they had known, I wanted them to unknow—or at least *feel* uncertain about. Where they had uncritical assumptions, I wanted to introduce questions. My hope was that they would be surprised by the Bible's depths, that they would wake up to its power to reorder their lives. I longed for the world of Scripture to seem foreign and

---

2. I was turned on to the relationship between love and witness through essays by Kevin Vanhoozer in *First Theology*. So I knew there was something there, even if I wasn't quite sure what. See Kevin J. Vanhoozer, *First Theology: God, Scripture and Hermeneutics* (Downers Grove, IL: InterVarsity Press, 2002).

3. Cut to small group leaders, nodding grimly.

4. We need appropriate reverence to explore the deep things of God. But we ought not let that calcify into a fearful foreclosing of our need for hermeneutical grace, either.

wonderful, to disrupt and put to death their platitudes and clichés.

We were not always so immune to the depths of things, so inoculated from the power and goodness around us that we may as well be asleep. As every child knows, the world is a miracle. When we first make our appearance, our home is a marvel and its corners and crannies contain a mystery. The most mundane objects become to children momentary sources of joy. And as children grow, their wonder and exploring take the form of questions, which children ask a lot of. One study found children who asked one to three questions *every minute*.[5] To the youngest among us, the world is a strange and fascinating place.

As we grow old, though, what once awed begins to irritate. Our sense of enchantment diminishes, as the world loses its charm and liveliness. We slowly give up on our exploring, leaving the adventures of learning and growth behind for the resigned, mildly despairing platitudes of "it is what it is" and "that's just who I am." The old adage that "familiarity breeds contempt" is little more than a rationalization for giving up and yielding to the weakness of a life without joy.

Good questions make the familiar seem strange to us. If we are willing to linger for a moment over the initial frustration of not immediately knowing the answer, we will find that a good question will revive our sense of wonder at the world. It is a joyful thing to be young again, to have our hearts revived with a sense of our own lack of understanding combined with an earnest desire to grow. As we return to our explorations, we find ourselves in a world not of our own making but a world that is good.

---

5. Yes, it was a small sample size, because counting questions from children is a difficult task.

THE FIRST STEP AWAY FROM HOME

"Home is where one starts from,"[6] T. S. Eliot wrote, which is an apt way of putting it. When we undertake an intellectual expedition, we have to begin from somewhere. We do not approach the world as though it is shapeless and void: we tacitly adopt a way of seeing things through our habits, traditions, and from our parents and peers. We start not as a blank slate but as people who have been formed to ask certain questions and ignore others. We begin our explorations inside an intellectual home.

It is true that intellectual homesteading has fallen into disrepute among certain "progressive" factions. Richard Dawkins, who has assumed the arch-atheist title, wondered in *The God Delusion* whether it might always be "a form of child abuse to label children as possessors of beliefs that they are too young to have thought about."[7]

The idea that children must make up their own minds on questions about religion is a fantasy, though. We quite reasonably start out without choosing all the beliefs we possess, largely because we don't "possess" beliefs in the way Dawkins's language suggests. We don't pick and choose them off the belief rack, as though they were bits of clothing that we don and doff with ease. We inhabit our beliefs and commitments, forming and reforming them through our interactions with the world and our critical reflection about it. They possess *us*, establishing a pattern for our lives and shaping our desires and dispositions.[8] That process simply isn't as straightforwardly conscious as Dawkins's question

---

6. Eliot, *Four Quartets*, 34.

7. Richard Dawkins, *The God Delusion* (Boston: Houghton Mifflin, 2006), 354. That this is even a question is interesting.

8. I think that the most important beliefs we have rarely, if ever, rise to the level of consciousness in anything other than a vague, inarticulate form. At least at the beginning. As we grow and learn to see more clearly, we learn to see those things, too.

makes it seem: we are acclimatized as children into presuming the world exists, a presupposition that no one is troubled with. The real worry folks like Dawkins have is not with indoctrination but with Christian doctrines. Indoctrination is unavoidable. But if Christianity's commitments turn out to be true, then his bleak outlook really is not.

In fact, those who are raised in a stable intellectual home will be more prepared to question well than those whose intellectual upbringing is piecemeal or nonexistent. Even imperfect upbringings can provide young people with a sense of identity and belonging. When we know well the place we come from, it is easier to face up to the unknown. Those who are raised in communities with strong identities, where to be a member of that community *means* approaching the world in a particular way, are often able to take more risks—including intellectual risks—than those whose formations are ambiguous or vague.

I remember well the first time someone told me I wasn't ready to ask a particular question. It was my freshman year in the Torrey Honors Institute and we were reading *The Odyssey*. I wanted to ask a question about the whole poem and the tutor bluntly told me I wasn't ready to think about that yet. I had more work to do, more pieces to add to my brittle framework about *The Odyssey* before I could approach the questions I wanted to. I remember feeling offended but also intrigued: no one had ever told me that some questions should be avoided until I had the capacity to explore them. My "intellectual home" about *The Odyssey* simply wasn't stable or robust. I couldn't ask very good questions because I hadn't read the story very well.

To put the point more directly, those who begin from stable and robust frameworks—even if they are not *completely* true—will be more capable of exploring new ideas than those who do not.

As Luigi Giussani writes, the student "can be genuinely open and truly sympathetic only if he feels, even unconsciously, a sense of total security."[9] If our cognitive homes prove less sturdy than they seemed while we were growing up in them, they can be torn down and replaced. But for that to happen, there must be a home first.

THE STRANGE WORLD OF CHRISTIANITY

My laugh began as a grin, but it slowly morphed into a belly roar. It was just before my sophomore year of college and I was somewhere north of Sacramento, driving the long road to Southern California. I was thinking about Christianity, as I had spent a good deal of time over the break arguing things out with my brother. As I considered the nature of Christianity's central claims—that Jesus was fully God and man, that the death of Jesus two thousand years ago somehow covered the wrongs I had done, and so on—the whole thing struck me as monstrously funny, as absurd to the point of ludicrous. I wasn't exactly "lost in wonder, love, and praise," but I was struck by an irrepressible sense of mirth. It's a strange world that we Christians believe in.

The world exists outside and before our inquiry into it. And it is an endlessly fascinating place. I mean, have you considered the massive range of meanings we can convey with just our eyebrows? I have stood outside cathedrals and looked at gargoyles, a part of architecture that I still don't understand. A friend of mine discovered a gene once. Octaves in music have ratios of 2:1, which if you ask me makes them a miracle. Do you know if you have two speakers "bumping" at the same wavelength, they can cancel each other out, so that you wouldn't hear a thing? Have you stood at the top of Niagara Falls and wondered how much water is rushing

---

9. Luigi Giussani, *The Risk of Education: Discovering Our Ultimate Destiny* (New York: Crossroad Pub., 2001), 62.

past you? Did you know some people have crossed it on a really tiny rope? Or plunged over it in a barrel? What moves a man to say, "Yes, this is the year I will climb into a two-foot wide ring of wood and go hurtling over a several-hundred foot waterfall"? What *is* man, and what sort of a fool can he be?

Romance is a mixture of "the familiar and the unfamiliar," G. K. Chesterton once put it.[10] Any intellectual framework that domesticates the world by refusing to recognize its strangeness will eventually run out of energy.[11] The most fulfilling, most romantic frameworks leave room for plenty of unknowns, yet unknowns that can be known *as* unknowns. Think about friendship: over the course of its life, we will discover a great deal about another person. Even though we are finite, our capacity for change leaves open the possibility that we may always learn more about each other. The other always remains an unknown whom we get to explore (and unknowns will always remain beyond us both, which we can explore together). When we live within the romantic tension of knowing and not knowing, our interests take us out into the world and we are able to experience the joy of learning, a joy that is never finished because there is always a deeper understanding available to us.

As Christians, our understanding of the world is good, true, and beautiful enough to keep us wondering forever. Like any good home, Christianity turns out to be delightfully odd and quirky, with idiosyncrasies and habits that seem downright strange to outsiders (baptism, anyone?) but that make some sense from within. Regardless of what happens in communion, folks taking a tiny wafer and a little bit of wine or grape juice is pretty odd, isn't it? And

---

10. G. K. Chesterton, *The Essential Gilbert K. Chesterton: Vol. I: Non-Fiction* (Radford, VA: Wilder, 2007), 8.

11. Plato's own philosophical system is a good example. It eventually dried up because it failed to see that the paradoxes went "all the way down," as it were.

those are only our practices: the God we worship took on human flesh, which as a fact is an infinite source of inquiry and praise.

But the romance is an adventure because our questions have consequences. The pursuit of truth and understanding is a grand drama, which may end as a comedy or not. When a man pursues a woman, he stands between marriage and refusal. But when he pursues an insight, he risks the possibility of being wrong. If it turns out that Jesus didn't rise from the dead, Christianity would unravel pretty quickly.[12] That is not a question that Christians explore with a "fifty-fifty" posture, as if it might be true or might not be. The beliefs and practices that make us Christians depend upon us starting from the assumption that the resurrection happened and pursuing the question from that stance. Of course, if we were to understand perfectly the resurrection and all the surrounding historical details, we would see all the reasons *against* it as well. But exploring those as possibilities is simply the drama of seeking understanding, a drama constituted by the possibility that we might end up on the wrong side of the ledger.

Sometimes our exploring moves us to leave our intellectual homes behind. We discover that planks in the raft are leaky or rotten, and that it can no longer take us across the sea like we hoped. Sometimes core parts of our framework *do* turn out to be wrong and their replacements introduce substantive changes to our lives. Such transitions often happen when people encounter evidence or questions that their own framework cannot resolve. The process may take the form of a crisis, or it may be a slow and long evolution of views. But intellectual conversions do occur and people move into newer and (they hope) more truthful confines.

My own core commitments have been relatively stable: in

---

12. It might seem at a particular moment to us that He did not and we would still be justified in believing it, of course. Questions are not always defeaters and having a belief *momentarily* defeated does not always mean you should instantly give it up.

fact, I am often surprised to remember how intuitions I had as a young man have been refined and honed as I have grown but not fundamentally altered or revised. Despite the overall constancy, some of the subtle shifts have reworked how I think about the world. I once emphasized the importance of making a difference right now and stressed our ability to fundamentally alter the character of society. But as I have explored the faithfulness of God's providence in the midst of hard times and the overturning of what the world expected in Christ's death on the cross, I have adopted a much more patient, long-term disposition. Rather than reaping a cultural harvest, I have turned my mind toward sowing seeds before the winter sets in. It is a subtle shift, but one that has significantly reoriented how I speak about the world and the sort of activities I invest in.

The language of "home" suggests that there are motivations *besides* our desire to know the truth that inspire our explorations. We want comfort and stability. We want the fellowship and community of friendship. We want the social esteem that comes from being affirmed by those we admire and respect. No conversion is *strictly* intellectual, because no framework can be abstracted from our lives in that way. But we were made for the comfort of intellectual stability and the friendships and unity that comes with those who share our outlook. At the end of all things, when Jesus takes us home, our most divisive questions will be answered and at least one disagreement will be no more (if not many others!). And that sort of unity is something we ought to all long for.

Even so, intellectual conversions feel like a sort of homelessness. Our framework orients us in the world: it is how we decide through our reflection and deliberation whether we will do this or that. Calling it into question destabilizes us; our sense of balance and place gets thrown off. And we lose our "insider" status in the communities that shared those commitments, which introduces a new level of unfamiliarity. Such periods of transition can be very difficult and feel very isolating. When I first began questioning in a substantive, serious way, my newfound disposition meant I no longer fit in as well with some of my previous friends. It is true that like an alcoholic coming upon drink I abused the method and needlessly caused offense. But while many relationships have mended, the gaps have remained real.

Every intellectual conversion is a repudiation of what came before. Unless we want to embrace a lazy sort of relativism and say that all perspectives are true, then there is no escaping the distance the change creates. Which is why a bit of Entishness ("Don't be hasty!") and a fair amount of gratitude for where we've come from would do us well. The potential for offense is always greater than we realize, and how we make our conversions is nearly as important as the conversions we undertake.

THE ORDER OF THE WORLD AND OF OUR QUESTIONS

"Nature gives most of her evidence," C. S. Lewis once wrote, "in answer to the questions we ask her."[13] Questions send us out into the world to find answers, but what "counts" as an answer is in a sense determined by the question we've asked. If we only pose scientific questions, then the world will deliver mechanistic results. If we ask psychological questions, then we may be primarily concerned with people's feelings and secondarily with what's transpiring in their brains. If we ask a historical question—how did *this* come to be?—then we shall find ourselves with historical answers. If we read Genesis and the only questions that come to

---

13. C. S. Lewis, *The Discarded Image: An Introduction to Medieval and Renaissance Literature* (Cambridge: University Press, 1964), 223.

mind are about science, then we set ourselves up to find answers that fit.

Questions also run in the opposite direction: sometimes, what we learn and discover moves questions to the edges or makes them unintelligible altogether. We once believed that the sun revolved around the earth. But the questions that generated that way of seeing have almost entirely been replaced. We have learned that the earth revolves around the sun and our questions now assume that knowledge. And so on for many other issues. Unless you're North Korea, that is, and are interested in manipulating people to buttress your pseudotheocratic regime. The state news outlet once reported that they'd found a unicorn lair.[14] They do that sort of thing every now and then to make their country seem better than it is so they can maintain their evil, iron-fisted control. But for everyone else in the world, the existence of unicorns is a question that is sufficiently closed.

The cost for North Korean–style manipulation is incredibly high. At some point reality intrudes on us or we experience the mental and social erosion that results from clinging to our artificial constructs. One can only believe in the Easter Bunny or Santa Claus for so long. Eventually, things will stop adding up and the belief will come crumbling down. But depending on the complexity of our framework and its proximity to the truth, it may take a lifetime (or longer) for those cracks to show. But show they someday will, for we have been made to integrate into reality and have reality integrated into us.

The world has an order, and the more we discern that order, the more fitting our questions will be. To question a dog as though

---

14. I really wish I was joking. But I'm not. See Eun Kyung Kim, "North Korea claims discovery of 'unicorn lair,'" *NBC Today News*, December 3, 2012. http://www. today.com/id/50058129/site/todayshow/ns/today-today_news/t/north-korea- claims-discovery-unicorn-lair/.

it were a human would be something of an intellectual *faux pas*. [15]
It would be the local equivalent of searching for unicorn stories to
support a tyrannical dictator, we might say. It would be bad form
to direct a question about nuclear physics toward a hummingbird
at the feeder. The question is well outside the given scene before
us. But to wonder about airspeed, or the varieties of birds, or the
ecological effects of birdseed, or what sort of food hummingbirds
prefer—the questions are there, embedded in the events that we
are witnessing if we are willing to patiently attend to them.

The order of the world, though, isn't easy to discern. And our
awareness of ambiguity often breeds questions in us. Consider
Mona Lisa and her ineffable countenance: the confounding nature
of her expression has launched a thousand dissertations and spec-
ulations. The combination of the portrait's simple beauty and the
uncertainty of her expression engenders a longing to understand
what the painting means.

Other ambiguities are more difficult to live with, though, especially moral ambiguities. We do not have the freedom to rumi-
nate and wonder when we must make a decision. Will we take
the job before us or not? What do we say to our friend who has
just told a lie? Will we offer forgiveness to those who have not
asked for it? Such questions occasionally (though mercifully, not
as often as they might!) intrude on our consciousness and demand
our attention.

But moral ambiguities also take a social form. Events sometimes render our understanding of the world implausible, which
is why the most pressing questions of our day are often different from those of previous generations. Where we wrestle with
the meaning of human life and the nature of human sexuality, the

---

15. Unless one happened to live in Narnia, or thought he lived in Narnia, or even
    thought there was a reasonable chance that this world could be Narnia—in which
    case, question away.

post–World War II world was confronted by the question of communism and the morality of nuclear weapons. How should we as a society treat those whose opinions offend us? What is marriage and who is able to partake in it? What sort of measures should a government take to protect its people? How shall we respond to terrorism? These are all questions that have been put before us in recent years, many of which we did not choose ourselves.

Because such questions are hard, we should hold all the more firmly to our commitment to finding answers. The paths of right and wrong through a given situation may initially not be clear. But because an answer is difficult to find does not mean one is impossible. The right way often requires deliberation and discernment of what the situation calls for. It requires patience and long-suffering and a reconsideration of our sources for guidance and instruction. We might sit with the wise and ask their advice. We ought to consider history to find analogous situations (while also paying careful attention to the ways situations differ). We would consider Scripture's narratives and pronouncements. But while doing our due diligence on the question before us, we should remember above all that the mercy of God covers our missteps and that the grace of God has not left our paths without light.

Consider the decisions that we face about whether we shall take a given job or turn it down. For young people particularly, who feel the weight of endless possibilities, the question of their job can evoke considerable anxieties. The path before us often seems ambiguous and shrouded in darkness. We often do not know what we want or what we want to do. We may have some conception of the sort of life we want to have, but little idea of how to bring it about. But by patiently deliberating, seeking counsel, and continuing to explore, we can slowly gain clarity on the vocation that God has called us to—even while resting within His providential care over our lives.

The irony is that punting and suggesting that there are "gray areas" that cannot be resolved into decisions that are "right" or "wrong" closes down questioning prematurely. Should a Christian ever drink alcohol or not? In the abstract, we will find plenty of ways of framing questions such that there is no claim on us. But we do not make decisions in the abstract: we are confronted by a particular situation, where there is enough outside information as to make a "gray area" totally implausible. While it may take years to discover the "right thing" on a particular moral question, a commitment to a fundamental moral order means that we do not have the luxury of quitting the search because we have found an "exception."[16] That is simply to excuse ourselves from the responsibility of gaining wisdom in a frequently confusing world. The commitment to a fundamental moral order keeps inquiry alive and strong.

THE GIVEN WORLD AND THE END OF CYNICISM

The world is not formless and void. It does not lie inert before us, waiting for us to make our own meaning by asserting our wills over it. Our questioning directs us away from ourselves, out toward the world. But before we inquire, there must be a world to be explored. I know that's an obvious point, but if we deny it, our inquiry will sound more like cynicism than love. Cynicism perpetually sees *through*. Understanding sees *how* and *why*. If our inquiry is oriented toward seeing the world, then we must at some point reach a level we can hold on to. As C. S. Lewis wrote:

---

16. Of course, as noted, not every situation allows for years of deliberation. But this is also why we reflect about our decisions—to discern the order and learn from them for the future.

The whole point of seeing through something is to see something through it. It is good that the window should be transparent, because the street or garden beyond it is opaque. How if you saw through the garden too? It is no use trying to "see through" first principles. If you see through everything, then everything is transparent. But a wholly transparent world is an invisible world. To "see through" all things is the same as not to see.[17]

Even if everything in creation dissolved into the ether, we would still be left with the Father, Son, and Holy Ghost, the "first principle" who makes possible any knowledge or understanding. To deny that means embracing a cynical skepticism, which frequently matures (rots?) into the vanity of an outright nihilism.

Because of our location inside the world—rather than as makers and rulers of it—our understanding can never be comprehensive. We are a part of the whole and we examine it from within, which necessarily limits our vision. The world encompasses us and not we the world. As (then) Joseph Ratzinger wrote, the world is "continually outstripping our capacity to *apprehend* and reaching out to a recognition of the way in which we are comprehended."[18]

To recognize that we are safely comprehended by goodness and order is to begin to feel at home. To "fit in" is an experience that goes beyond familiarity. We may be familiar with a colleague without ever feeling quite at home with him. The experience of being at home completes us. We are genuinely free to be ourselves. There is no understating the sort of satisfaction that results in: to feel as though we have "found our place" is to experience a profound and rare good.

---

17. C. S. Lewis, *The Abolition of Man, or, Reflections on Education with Special Reference to the Teaching of English in the Upper Forms of Schools* (New York: HarperCollins, 2001), 81.

18. Pope Benedict XVI, *Introduction to Christianity*, 47.

Our sense of being "at home" comes and goes, and will until Jesus returns. One of the strongest times when I've felt it was the night I proposed to my wife. I was particularly anxious about everything and so asked Jesus for a unique sense of calm. I can't point to many specific prayers in my life that were unambiguously answered, but this was one. As I knelt before her, a remarkable awareness that all was well came over me—a peace that transcended understanding, you might say. All I knew in that moment was that her "yes" had brought the world to a halt, that I would be able to face any suffering or sorrow.[19]

As Christians, we come to our rest by acknowledging that all things have already been comprehended by God and that they have been given us in Christ. "All things are yours," Paul tells us, because we are Christ's and Christ is God's. Our particular lines of inquiry may lead us to the outer reaches of the cosmos or the deepest corners of the soul. But in each direction we explore territory that has already been marked out by another.

We can explore the world, in other words, because God made it and in His gracious providence has given us the freedom to enjoy it. There is no place where we can escape His presence: He is the One in whom we "live, move, and have our being." To use a common medieval formula, God is an infinite sphere whose center is everywhere and whose circumference does not exist. His presence locates all things and makes them intelligible to us, and in seeing the universe as *created*, we also see that it has been given by God to us. The confession that God is Creator is the ground from which we understand the world.

The paradox of Christianity is that when we set out to explore the things of God, we discover that all else good and beau-

---

19. I do not often speak thus: We find ourselves at this moment somewhere near the borders of language.

tiful is thrown in as well. In the incarnation and resurrection of Jesus Christ, we are transformed and made as solid as He is, even as we wait for the final glorification of our bodies and the permanent renewal of creation. Our cynical detachment, our despairing skepticism, our obfuscating retreat into grayness and ambiguity—these too will pass when we finally see our Savior "face-to-face."

We will one day finally be permanently at home in the universe because God first came as a stranger into it. And the more we walk in His footsteps, the more at rest we can be. Even now, within the light Scripture, we can see partially, incompletely, and dimly—we see men, but still dimly, like trees. But we are still seeing. And by bringing our inquiry in conformity to our confession, our vision is trained so that we are ready for that great day when we shall finally encounter our Savior face-to-face.

6

The Liberation of
Questioning

———————— ❧ ————————

Would not the beggar then forget himself?
—TAMING OF THE SHREW[1]

When I was in high school, my relationship with my youth pastor was tenuous. It was a rocky road for us, which was mostly my fault. As the pastor's son, I was a terror in Bible studies. It wasn't simply that I thought I was right, though I often did. I was self-consciously striving to know more about the Bible than anyone else in the room and was always pleased to demonstrate my knowledge when the opportunity arose.

It was a Sunday morning and our little group was trudging through the doctrine of the Holy Spirit. Our youth pastor was a recent college graduate who could have made a good living as a professional drummer. That morning, he made a point of reminding us that the Holy Spirit didn't arrive around these parts until Pentecost.

---

1. William Shakespeare, *The Complete Works of William Shakespeare* (Ware, England: Wordsworth Editions, 2007), 329.

Until that point in our relationship, most of my questions had stemmed from my desire to woo pretty girls who loved Jesus by demonstrating my keen biblical insight.[2] This time, though, I experienced a bit of genuine confusion. The facts simply didn't fit the theory, as they say, so I piped up: "But if the Holy Spirit didn't come to earth at all until Pentecost, how can David plead in Psalm 51 not to have the Holy Spirit taken away from him?" I didn't doubt my youth pastor's teaching. I simply didn't understand it. It was quite possibly the only real question I asked in all my high school years.

My inquiry did not go over well. With a sharp tone, he abruptly told me to go ask my father, who was the senior pastor.[3] And then he moved on. But the moment left a mark. Two things were strikingly clear: he had no idea how to answer my question and he clearly felt it was a challenge to his authority.

Our questions are inseparable from our histories. They don't simply float above us, angel-like in the ether. They are tied to the stories of our lives and the habits and practices of thought that have formed us. We have *this* particular interest in part because we were formed in *that* particular way. Had I not been (happily) raised in a biblically literate household, the question never would have occurred to me. And had I not earned for myself a reputation of being pretentious, I suspect my youth pastor might not have been so curt.

Questioning is rooted in what we love, in the goods we consciously and unconsciously orient our lives around and aim our desires toward. Growing up, my questions were frequently motivated not by an interest in the answer *per se* but by my eagerness to impress. And, to be candid, I worry that many of them still are.

---

2. This was strangely unsuccessful, prompting my first serious inquiry into whether God is good.

3. Which I did that night. And we had a good conversation about things, wherein he was very helpful. Thanks, Dad.

Having recently returned to school for a graduate degree, I have been simultaneously terrified and fascinated by how easily my ambition, rather than my desire for understanding in itself, motivates my pursuits.

As a form our loves take, questioning faces all the corruption and corrosion that happens in a sinful world. We cannot assume intellectual purity, especially of ourselves. All that we ask and all that we don't ask are called into question, as beneath our questions lie desires that may themselves be disordered. Just as our love for people has its lustful distortions, so also do our love and desire for truth.

Such misguided loves shape the communities we inhabit, which then conversely reinforce those loves. My own prideful posturing and my youth pastor's authoritarian dismissal stood in the way of our ability to inquire together. He had no eyes to see the sincerity of my confusion, and I was frustrated he couldn't detect it. But our miscommunication also made questioning more difficult for everyone else. As someone with some influence on my peers, my pseudoquestioning created an environment where truth wasn't valued for its own sake. And my youth pastor's insecurities made it harder for him to see when questions were subversive and when they were not, which meant only the approved questions could be asked.

Questioning needs to be liberated. We can't simply take up inquiry as part of our formation without seeing the ways in which it too has become entangled in a fallen heart and the structures of a fallen world. If we fail to orient the practice appropriately—around the gracious actions of God and His authorized witness to them—then we will simultaneously fail to cultivate the virtues and communities that we need in order to question well.[4]

---

4. I deal with the communal dimension of inquiry in the next chapter.

Set Free from Defensiveness

The first public talk I gave after writing my book on the physical body was in a well-educated and wealthy community. I was examining various practices like yoga and plastic surgery, which were popular in the surrounding area, to see how they relate to specifically religious practices like prayer and fasting. And then someone asked a question that I knew might come but didn't know quite how to answer: Is there a way to specify some practices (like prayer) as "uniquely Christian" while ruling out others (like yoga) without dividing the world into the "sacred" and the "secular"? In my talk, I had tried to straddle both sides: we shouldn't divide the sacred from the secular but we *should* treat prayer differently from yoga. How do those two hold together?

When the question came, I could feel the entire room lean forward with interest. It wasn't a "gotcha" question. It simply highlighted a perceived inconsistency. I knew it and the entire room knew it. In that moment, I felt every temptation to respond defensively and blow off the question or simply obfuscate and deflect. The question threatened the integrity of my talk, and I wanted to preserve my own sense of being an authority. Yet I also knew that the question is a fundamental one once we start thinking about the body. So I instead overruled my defensiveness, complimented the question, and then tackled it.[5] I didn't make much headway that evening, but it didn't much matter. We had a great conversation regardless.

Sometimes questions unsettle us at levels that we can't quite name. After all, our beliefs are more than a "worldview," a term that makes it look like we look through our beliefs like we look out the window. Some of our beliefs are central to our self-understanding: they stand with, in, and around our form of life. Removing them

---

5. I don't know if I was successful in that, it should be noted. Sometimes I tell myself I'm inquiring only to realize later that my real interest was defense.

would be more akin to heart surgery than a change of clothing; it would leave a deep scar and profoundly reshape our possibilities.[6] Our Christian faith is of this sort: it goes deep enough that we become "new creations." Such faith is more than a set of ideas: it creates a new presence in the world, one that pervades our bodies and souls. We don't *have* a worldview as Christians. We look out at the world as those who have been made new.

It's not surprising, then, that we are instinctively protective about our fundamental commitments and the self-understandings that emerge from them. Such commitments are familiar to us. We may have grown up with them. We think that they are true. And they have served us reasonably well.[7] When a question makes our core commitments seem strange or untrue, we feel uncomfortably disoriented. Even if our livelihood or public perception of us isn't at stake, our history, purposes, and self-perception probably are. Defensiveness isn't the appropriate response. But it is understandable.

Defensiveness isn't confidence, even though it often mimics it. The defensive temperament is grounded in the fear we might be wrong, rather than the "fear not" of the gospel.[8] It is not a sign of our belief's vitality but its frailty. It suggests we think our lives are at stake, that if we are wrong, it will be fatal. Such a mindset does not accord with a confident Christian life. As Christians, we do not possess the truth; we live within it and are possessed by it. Our primary role is as witnesses: we are "not the light" but

---

6. Romans 4:17 is a key verse in this regard, as is 2 Corinthians 5:17.

7. I speak broadly here, not only of Christians. There is an undercurrent in some people's rhetoric that faith makes people distinctively anti-intellectual. However, we should note that Christians don't seem to blame for the Hollywood entertainment industrial complex, which is probably the central locus of intellectual formation in America.

8. What we are worried will happen if we are wrong is often vague. And generally so are the questions. Fear breeds among the shadows, not in open sunlight.

"bear witness to the light."[9] Even when such a witness requires us to contend and draw the sharp lines between truth and error, we can do so without being motivated by the anxieties of defensiveness. The Christ to whom we bear witness willingly suffered the "defeat" of the cross out of His confidence in the faithful power of God. Within His life we have nothing to fear—even losing or being wrong, for neither state can endure long.

Defensiveness is a misguided form of asserting our own assurance. As I have talked with people, I have noticed that my most defensive moments are when my own interpretations or insights are at stake. I still am willing to argue vociferously for the stances and positions I have inherited from others. But my sense is that I do so with a good deal less reactionary defensiveness. I suspect the difference is that I do not think my inherited positions are "mine" in quite the same way as those I discover or invent. The notion that God became man is no more "mine" than the notion that twice two is four. But if someone questioned the latter, I'd have a good laugh and then go on my way. Chesterton's line that he did not make orthodoxy but that orthodoxy made him seems perfectly fitting. When we stake our lives on the truth, we stand on that which is outside of our heads, which means our assurance doesn't depend on what we can recall at any given moment. If we lean too heavily on the arguments and reasons we have at hand, we are internalizing the Christian faith in such a way that the proper grounds for our assurance are marginalized in our thinking, namely, the historical act of faithfulness to God's covenant by His Son, Jesus Christ.

Our assurance as Christians is not rooted in our own knowledge and love of God but in God's knowledge and love of us. Paul prays that the Philippians' love would "abound still more and

9. John 1:7–8 NIV.

more in real knowledge and all discernment," which suggests they have some of both. But three times Paul flips the formula on its head and points to God's knowledge of us as the grounds for the Christian life. My favorite is Galatians 4:9, where he writes, "But now that you have come to know God, *or rather to be known by God* . . ."[10] It's almost as though Paul catches himself and wants to make sure the order is right. In 1 Corinthians 8:3, Paul uses the same formula: "If anyone loves God, he is known by God." And in one of the key passages that points both to our knowledge of God now and the perfection of that knowledge later, Paul writes: "For now we see in a mirror dimly, but then face to face. Now I know in part; then I shall know fully, *even as I have been fully known.*"[11]

Our confidence in God's knowledge of us—our assurance—takes as its source the love of God as demonstrated in history at the cross. In the person of Jesus, we are encountered by a God who shared every part of humanity. In Jesus' sacrificial love we find mercy for all our intellectual sins and errors, for those questions we ask badly and those we do not ask at all. The cross sets our questioning free by instilling in us the courage to inquire by removing any reason for fear. We are free within the confines of the cross to love God and ask what we want.[12]

The cross also promises freedom from the defensiveness that so many of us feel in the face of difficult or hostile questions. Throughout the gospel of Matthew, Jesus engages in questioning jujitsu with the religious leaders who opposed Him. Their questions come as traps and tests, and Jesus counters with queries of His own. In Matthew 22 Jesus proves Himself victorious at the questioning gamesmanship by asking one that the religious lead-

---

10. Emphasis mine (ESV).

11. 1 Corinthians 13:12 (ESV). Emphasis mine.

12. Modifying Augustine's famous dictum, which is found in his seventh homily on 1 John.

ers cannot answer. The episode concludes with Matthew's mildly chilling, mildly hilarious remark, "nor from that day did anyone dare to ask him any more questions."[13]

Yet the religious leaders' opposition does not end even though the dialogue does. Instead, naked hostility replaces the trickery of subversive questioning. At His trial, Jesus is examined for claiming to be the Son of God. Rather than engage the lawyers, Matthew repeatedly notes Jesus' silence before them. His recurring response is, "You have said so," which is all He tells Pilate before judgment is passed.[14] He makes no long protestation or defense on His own behalf, offers no apologia for the rationality or truthfulness of His stance. As Isaiah put it earlier, "Like a lamb that is led to the slaughter . . . he opened not his mouth."[15]

Yet Jesus also demonstrates no fear because He had resolved it elsewhere. Jesus communicates His desire that the cup of His suffering should pass Him by through speaking with God in the garden prior to His trial. Making His fears known to God gives Jesus serene and implacable confidence before men. The disciples are advised earlier in the gospel that when they are dragged before "governors and kings . . . what you are to say will be given to you in that hour." Apparently we will sometimes be so confident that we will not need say anything at all.[16]

The hurried rush to defend ourselves often indicates a lack of confidence in God. When we are safe and secure in the hands of Jesus, even those questions that are veiled attacks will neither trouble nor disturb us. Sometimes we ought to speak in response—as Paul does before Felix in Acts 24—but such speaking

---

13. Matthew 22:46 (ESV).

14. Matthew 26:64 (ESV).

15. Isaiah 53:7 (ESV).

16. Paul is another witness, of course. And when he goes before Agrippa, he says quite a bit. Which is worth bearing in mind before we reject speaking altogether.

will be constituted by a cheerful disregard for our own security and life because the truth that we proclaim has the power of life over death. It is precisely because Paul so eagerly desires the "fellowship of [Christ's] sufferings" that he is free from the sort of defensive posture of those who desperately cling to their lives.[17]

Set Free from Self-Sufficiency

What would we do if all the answers were delivered from heaven and all our questions disappeared overnight? Would we welcome the answers as a gift and go on living to the praise of God's glory? Or would we harbor a secret discontentment that we'd been cheated out of our questions? For some of us, the prospect of having all our inquiries answered is more frightening than it might seem. We spend a good deal of time as North American Christians arguing about the church's position in the world and her urgent need for reform. We have an industry of critique making and solution selling. Various networks of books, blogs, and conferences exist to help Christians respond to the tide of secularism, rehabilitate the church's teaching of the gospel, take Christianity back from the religious right, or cure whatever the latest ailment happens to be.

As someone who has engaged in my own version of that project, I sometimes wonder where we would be if things actually changed. What would we write about if there were no more problems to solve? Would I be okay if "my voice" became superfluous?[18] Were all our efforts to come to fruition, would we be as enthusiastic about the results as we are when our criticisms find a hearing?

It is possible to love our questions more than their answers.

---

17. Philippians 3:10 (NASB).

18. Some would say it already is superfluous. They are closer to the kingdom than they realize.

Questioning is invigorating, once you acclimatize to it. There's constantly something new to explore, some new insight to glean. The whole mode is downright thrilling. But it's love that marks Christians off as the people of God and love that should guide our questioning. Not an amorphous, undirected, ambiguous impulse that makes us feel warm and fuzzy inside but a love defined by the sharp edges of Jesus' life and the creed. "We believe in one God, the Father Almighty" is the answer at the heart of the Christian's confession, an answer that is the root of our being and the wellspring of all our energy.

If Christianity were a series of endless questions, it would amount to no more than Platonism. Answers liberate questioning by allowing us to rest. The burden of exploration is too heavy for us to carry, which is why most of us abandon it. But if we allow ourselves to question with no hope of answers, we will someday reach exhaustion. As the author of Ecclesiastes put it, "I applied my heart to seek and to search out by wisdom all that is done under heaven. It is an unhappy business that God has given to the children of man to be busy with."[19] This is the same God who "has put eternity into man's heart, *yet so that he cannot find out what God has done from the beginning to the end.*"[20]

In the early church, the confession of the creeds would often take the form of a call and response. What do you believe? "We believe in one God." Pronouncing our commitment isn't the end of our exploration but questioning's renewal and liberation. Questioning can be a form of self-justification and rationalization, of trying to find out the answers ourselves so that we no longer stand in need of grace. Yet when we live within the creed, we repeatedly acknowledge and confess our need for help. When the answer of our justification is given to us in Christ, we still learn

---

19. Ecclesiastes 1:13 (ESV).
20. Ecclesiastes 3:11 (ESV). Emphasis mine.

and inquire and grow. But we can let go of the burden of imitating omniscience, for those in Christ have been justified already.

The paradox is that the moment we reduce our lives to questioning and inquiry, we lose the reason for our exploring. Questioning is not able to sustain itself on its own—it is justified by the end it orients us toward and grounded in the love by which we move there.

SET FREE FROM CURIOSITY

We do not speak often of the *vice* of curiosity anymore, but perhaps it is time for a retrieval. Of all the corrosions of the love of understanding, curiosity may be the most pervasive and subsequently the hardest to detect. As a vice, curiosity respects no boundaries around the desire to know. Questions of timing and appropriateness are irrelevant to the curious; they are motivated to attain the mental stimulation of novelty more than the good of understanding. As Paul Griffiths writes, curiosity differs from studiousness:

> Curiosity is concerned with novelty: curious people want to know what they do not yet know, ideally what no one yet knows. Studious people seek knowledge with the awareness that novelty is not what counts, and is indeed finally impossible because anything that can be known by any one of us is already known to God and has been given to us as unmerited gift.[21]

While curiosity seems admirable, the paradox is that those moved by it cannot abide the unknown. What postures as a love of inquiry would lead to, if unrestrained, the extinction of exploration. As Augustine writes, "It is more accurate to say that [the curious] hate the unknown because they want everything to

---

21. Paul J. Griffiths, *Intellectual Appetite: A Theological Grammar* (Washington, DC: Catholic University of America Press, 2009), 21–22.

become known, and thus nothing to remain unknown."[22] The studious, however, have a love for knowledge that welcomes it as a gift. They do not comprehend or possess the world by knowing it; their posture is not one of grasping and claiming but of joyfully receiving.

Ours is a world dominated by the cataloging of knowledge, by the searching out of the corners of the universe in order to find out its secrets. We have sent a rover to Mars, after all, and named it *Curiosity*. We have democratized the encyclopedic mindset through Wikipedia, giving us all instant access to all the information we could possibly want. In such an environment, emphasizing God's unknowability and transcendence—that He is beyond ultimate explanation—seems like an appropriate counterreaction. Yet the emphasis stands in danger of overcompensating by insisting that God cannot be understood *at all* by His creatures, even in the ways He has ordained to reveal Himself. The result can be a loose, nearly nihilistic emphasis on God's mysteriousness that perpetually sees (or rather, *posits*) a God behind the God who has given Himself to us in Jesus. The trick is to hold together the unknown with the knowing, the mystery with the revelation, the hidden with the gift.

Culturally, curiosity has been turbocharged by the omnipresent, omnipotent Internet. Whereas studiousness is comfortable with not knowing, those who are curious have a kind of restlessness. The thirst to know what is happening elsewhere, regardless of whether anything in our lives actually depends upon it, creates an information-oriented community that slowly and imperceptibly erodes the patience and silence that studiousness thrives in. As Thomas Aquinas puts it, "curiosity does not lie in the knowing

---

22. St. Augustine, *De Trinitate*, 10.1.3, quoted in Griffiths, *Intellectual Appetite*, 19.

precisely, but in the appetite and hankering to find out."[23] The pursuit of novelty is endless: memes are created, thrive, and die in hours. And curators race to compile and promote amusing and trivial links and pictures to temporarily sate the insatiable thirst to witness things we have never seen before (especially when kittens are involved).[24]

The advent of social media has only compounded the problem. When our path into the vast landscape began with search engines, our activity at least began with an end in mind. It's a pretty typical experience for me to set out looking for a particular quote from G. K. Chesterton that I half remember only to find myself somewhere in the ballpark of medieval theology. One thing leads to the next, and before I know it I've forgotten my original interest and picked up a new thread. But I at least began with a direction. When we start with social media, we often encounter a barrage of information that we didn't even know we cared about until we saw it and won't care much about the moment it passes. Videos of kids doing cute things? Why, absolutely! The news *autotuned*? Okay, why not? The endless trivialities thrust before us by friends and colleagues are like crack for the curious.

Curiosity stays on the surface of things. The moment the unknown becomes known, it is ready to move on. The curious are unable to linger and seek understanding, which means they have a tendency toward the superficial and the fleeting. At one time, *Trivial Pursuits* was simply a diversionary board game. But as long as curiosity deforms our intellectual desires, we can be sure that our pursuits will struggle to reach down to the crucial questions on which our lives depend.

---

23. Thomas Aquinas and Thomas Gilby, *Summa Theologica: Vol. 44, Well-Tempered Passion (2a2ae. 155–70)* (London: Blackfriars, 1972), question 167, article 1.
24. Buzzfeed is precisely what a curious generation wants—and deserves.

Set Free by Waiting

It is not until the end of all things that we shall know fully. It is ours not to grasp at that knowledge, to claim it like the curious, but to wait patiently with the growing confidence that it will be given to us in due time. Hopeful waiting for the consummation of knowledge sets our questioning free. In T. S. Eliot's *Four Quartets*, he writes:

> I said to my soul, be still and wait without hope
> For hope would be hope of the wrong thing.
> Be still, and wait without love
> For love would be love of the wrong thing.
> There is yet faith, but the faith, the hope, and the love
> Are all in the waiting. [25]

"Ask and it shall be given" is the promise. And all the promises of God are "yes and amen." But there is no timeline for their fulfillment. And many times when we pose our deepest and most pressing questions to God, we are brought into the heart-wrenching waiting that purifies our souls.

Waiting is never easy. But if answers are gifts, we cannot demand them. We have no entitlement, no claim on God such that He owes us answers for His actions or inaction. By assuming a posture of trustful waiting, we surrender our requirement that God meet us on our terms and open ourselves to His questioning of us. We learn in our waiting to respect God's freedom, to remember that God is a *person* and not an answer or favor dispensing machine.

Yet we often feel the absence of God more deeply and pervasively than we can say. We long not for a proposition but a presence. The psalm that best captures it for me is Psalm 13, which I replicate in full so as to not minimize its force:

25. Eliot, *Four Quartets*.

How long, oh Lord? Will you forget me forever?
How long will you hide your face from me?
How long must I take counsel in my soul
And have sorrow in my heart all the day?
How long shall my enemy be exalted over me?
Consider and answer me, O Lord my God;
Light up my eyes, lest I sleep the sleep of death,
Lest my enemy say, "I have prevailed over him,"
Lest my foes rejoice because I am shaken.
But I have trusted in your steadfast love;
My heart shall rejoice in your salvation.
I will sing to the Lord,
Because he has dealt bountifully to me.

What begins with a question ends in singing. Like the psalms I have mentioned elsewhere, this one, too, turns to affirming the "steadfast love" that remains despite appearances. But the time between the question and the presence is waiting and hope, waiting and expectation, waiting and pleading and prayer.

Waiting expectantly is not passivity; when we wait, we redirect our attention away from the immediacy of our situation and toward God Himself. We orient our lives toward the promise and live within its domain. Waiting is a posture of the heart that establishes an atmosphere of trustful dependence regardless of the activities we are called to undertake.

As a theme, waiting on God pervades the Psalms and Prophets. The most famous is probably from Isaiah 40:

Even youths shall faint and be weary,
and young men shall fall exhausted;
but they who wait for the Lord shall renew
    their strength;
they shall mount up with wings like eagles;

> they shall run and not be weary;
> they shall walk and not faint. [26]

Waiting upon the Lord may feel like despair and darkness, but it is in waiting that our youthful vitality finds its renewal. Yet the renewal often comes through pain and mortification. Cultivating a dependency upon God for "answers" often involves confronting the sinfulness of our hearts. We do not see, in part, because we are not ready to see: we have not the "purity of heart" that is necessary for our sense of God's absence to be replaced by the gloriousness of God's presence. Consider Psalm 130, which frames waiting in the context of the psalmist's confrontation with sin:

> If you, O Lord, should mark iniquities,
> O Lord, who could stand?
> But with you there is forgiveness,
> that you may be feared.
> I wait for the Lord, my soul waits,
> and in his word I hope;
> my soul waits for the Lord
> more than watchmen for the morning,
> more than watchmen for the morning. [27]

Our eager longing and expectation for God cannot be divorced from the word of His faithfulness to us. We look expectantly for the marks of His presence, training our eyes to see "the goodness of the Lord in the land of the living." We make our confession and our inquiries, pleading and prodding God to purify

---

26. Isaiah 40:30–31 (esv).
27. Psalm 130:3–5 (esv).

the eyes of our hearts that we might see Him.[28]

Hope is the mark of those who explore well; long-suffering is the heart of the healthy questioning life. As we linger over all that we know while patiently and quietly pleading for the unknowns to be made manifest, our lives will reverberate with confidence in the promises of God. The answers to our deepest questions do not always reveal themselves with the speed or ease we might demand—which is a fact of joy and not of despair to those who live within the promise. The same God who will not allow us to be tempted beyond what we can bear will also only give us the knowledge we can handle.[29]

Saying that answers "reveal themselves," though, is a slightly odd way of putting it, I realize. But that's what happens. Consider *Tree of Life,* which is a plodding and mysterious film. Its dialectical narration and poetic imagery are nothing like the straightforward, plot-based movies that we typically enjoy. The film doesn't quite raise questions—it clubs us with them. The answers are (I think) all there, but they are left hidden and opaque. It's almost as though filmmaker Terrence Malick has created a work that only those with ears to hear are able to understand.

I don't have answers to all my questions about *Tree of Life*—what *is* that attic about, anyway?—but the only place I'll find answers is within the work itself.[30] The film is a whole—it has a beginning, a middle, and an end, with layers of music and images and dialogue that all interrelate. As we wait for an answer, we take the whole into ourselves and sit with it, reflecting on its various com-

---

28. The above selections are only the beginning of the theme. See also Pss. 25:1–5; 27:13–14; 31:23–24; 33:20–22; 37; 38:13–16; 39:7–8; 40; 62; 69:2–3; Proverbs 20:22; Isaiah 8:16–18; Isaiah 25:9; Isaiah 30:18; Isaiah 33:2; Isaiah 51:5; Lamentations 3:22–27 (this one is particularly good); Micah 7:7; Zephaniah 3:8; Hebrews 6:15 and 9:28; James 5:7–9.

29. Cf. 1 Corinthians 10:13 and John 16:12.

30. And even if Malick were to provide the answer, we would still need to see it within the work itself in order for it to be properly understood.

ponents and seeing various relationships emerge. We might catch a glimpse of the film's meaning—but then we are sent back into the process of reflecting and waiting and working through the parts in their relationship to the whole. The process takes us deeper into the work. As we wait patiently and diligently consider, eventually more of the meaning will emerge before us.

Internalizing a work like *Tree of Life* is a soul-expanding exercise. There are some films and books (and Scripture is unquestionably one!) that I simply don't think my soul is yet large enough to contain—the questions they provoke are too large, too expansive, too devastating to me. *The Brothers Karamazov* is one, as is Charles Williams's *Descent into Hell*. It is almost impossible for me to linger because I feel overwhelmed by their immensity. The incorporation of the whole and the attempt to grasp their meaning leaves me with glimpses, but nothing more. Moments of recognition come— "Aha!"—and then fade, not because they are false but only because they are taken up into yet another layer of inquiry. I find myself with such texts confronted by the frailty of my own vision: I see men walking about as trees but lack the strength to see the rest.

There are some goods so immense and fundamental that to take them into ourselves would require our death. The tragic beauty of the cross—a God whose love and forgiveness enters a world where infants die, where children are sometimes killed in schools, where women are abused—the words fail right at this moment. It is true, as John the Baptist said, that "I must decrease and he increase." But the "increase" costs us everything, for the one who unites himself with Christ will also find himself hanged on a tree. To take this terrible good into our lives is to enter into death and through it, the life of Christ.[31]

Waiting upon *this* God undoes our world. His story makes us,

---

31. So in baptism we die with Christ.

not the other way around: "For I have died, and my life is hidden in Christ with God." "To live is Christ and to die is gain." "Come and die," Christ bids us. In surrendering our demand for answers and waiting for them to be given, we submit our questioning to the one who has searched out all things. Our exploring happens in the shadow of the cross, which is a judgment that makes us questionable while manifesting the answer of God.

But by questioning our questions, the cross sets them free. Questioning interposes a gap between ourselves and our beliefs, which makes us strangers and unknown to ourselves. Such a distancing is a form of death, as the question brings us to the end of ourselves by focusing our attention on what we are *not*.[32] That sort of exploration, though, is liberated when we live within God's knowledge of us, a knowledge that extends even to our sinfulness in Christ's work on the cross. We are free to be strangers to ourselves precisely because God is intimate with us, because He is *God with us*, because He has been God with us in the passion and resurrection of Jesus Christ.

All that the Lord sets free, He sets free to love. But love has a bloody purpose: it impels us to carry our cross and deny ourselves, to bring all under the lordship of Christ so that we can receive it back (and more) as a gift. No part of us is safe from this judgment, not even the commitments that form the backbone of our self-understanding. Such beliefs may be true, but not truthfully held. We may affirm them out of our fear, our envy, or the desire for our own advancement. But God seeks structural integrity all the way throughout our intellectual homes: "Thou desirest truth in the inward parts,"[33] is David's prayer. As we incorporate the authorized witness to Christ's life into our souls and allow it to

---

32. Which is partly why Plato thought that the work of philosophy was preparation for our own deaths.

33. Psalm 51:6 (KJV).

infiltrate our lives, we will find its questions and answers undoing and rebuilding our lives on a more firm foundation.

Questioning is liberated when we do not ask it to do too much. Reality makes us; we do not make it. And at the heart of reality, out of the silence of unknowing emerges the cross. The cross engenders within us the courage to explore without finding, to wait without an answer, to search without seeing—precisely because we know one has already gone before us into death, come back victorious from it, and will come again to consummate His triumph over sin. Our questioning is liberated, ultimately, by the "assurance of things hoped for, the conviction of things not seen." But until then, we place our understanding on the altar and wait for it to be burned up or given back, as Isaac was given back to Abraham.[34] It is not in this country that we will find the end of our exploring but the country that has been prepared for us—a country that we will know with all the strange romantic familiarity of those who have arrived to a home that encompasses within it the universe and that they have been to before.

---

34. And all that is false shall be burned up like dross.

7

Communities of
Inquiry

———— ⌒ ————

"Is America a Christian nation?"

The question came through a translator and took me by surprise. I had been teaching online for Underground University, which provides biblical training for North Korean refugees. I had spent four weeks talking about the intersection of theology and the physical body and this was my final class. And even though the question had nothing to do with anything I had said, I was grateful for it.

For the most part, students had sat through my classes with what seemed to me total indifference. North Koreans are generally not physically expressive in their manner, as we in North America are. But they also grow up under a regime by which questions are regarded as necessarily subversive and an affront to the

---

1. John Steinbeck, *East of Eden* (New York: Penguin Books, 2002), 25.

teacher's authority. To ask a question is a sign of disrespect and in a state run school might be dangerous. When I mentioned the question to the director of the program, he was surprised that anyone had spoken up at all.

The North Korean regime *has* to teach that questions undermine authority because the moment they allow them to be asked, their elaborately constructed lies will begin to unravel. The surest way to maintain power is to make sure no one thinks. "What a tangled web we weave," is the old saying, "when first we practice to deceive." The moment people begin questioning, such webs are in trouble. [2]

The gospel sets questioning free in a way that the North Korean government could never do. They are a unique situation: they have complete political control and virtually no restrictions on how they treat their people. And their power depends upon throttling and controlling the questions people ask. But within the justifying work of Christ, we are set free to ask our questions even if we are not immediately given the answers. A regime predicated on lies must fear the truth and those who seek it. But a faith that is really and ultimately true need fear nothing—even questions that are as subversive as the serpent's.

Whether we are in North Korea or a North American church, our inquiries take shape within the communities in which we live and are shaped by them. [3] The virtues and vices that we exhibit in our questioning are often embedded in the communities that form us. And we do not pose our questions in a vacuum. Those we live with may be more or less welcome to them, more or less able to reflect critically on their own presuppositions and commitments

---

2. We tend to overestimate our own and other people's abilities to live successfully within lies. Yet it seems one lesson from collapses like Enron, many cults, Lance Armstrong, Tiger Woods, and others is that eventually the truth will find us out, regardless of how many resources we have to expend on keeping up appearances. North Korea will not be a totalitarian regime forever.

3. I should note that the comparison is strictly at the level that both take social form as institutions, and nothing more.

if they are called into question.

We can't escape entanglements with others as we explore our world. And we shouldn't want to. While some churches may be inhospitable to those who doubt or wrestle with their faith, we explore best when we learn to question with others.

THE SACRIFICE OF QUESTIONING

We often think about inquiry with an individualistic cast of mind. After all, it is often *our* understanding that we are most interested in pursuing and *our* awareness of the negative spaces that feels the most pressing to us. This is especially true when our questions arise from the experience of suffering or the purgative fires of loneliness. As I mentioned earlier, we start our explorations from where we are—and that usually means beginning with concerns that are rooted in our personal histories and experiences. But we cannot stay there.

I remember well my first conversation at the Torrey Honors Institute. At the end of our first session together, the professor remarked that we would have real conversations when we began to care about each other's learning more than our own. It was a simple point, taken straight from Scripture's admonition to look not only to our own interests but the interests of others.[4] I took the advice to heart. From that point on, I treated our conversations as microcosms of my life, which meant striving to follow other people's concerns rather than seek my own.

If we are clinging to our need for answers, then we will struggle to lay down our pursuits for the good of others. If all we can feel is the existential angst of our own uncertainties, then it will be hard to attend to other people's concerns. If our explorations are paths of our self-justification, then we never learn to

---

4. Philippians 2:4 (ESV).

lay aside our own learning and carry the cross of someone else's. The euphoria of an epiphany has an intoxicating quality; it is like an explosion of joy and those who have tasted it once can easily be addicted to it and base their lives on it. Such a pleasure isn't wrong: if anything, that it accompanies learning is partly because encountering the truth is a fundamental human good. But to sacrifice such a good for the sake of another is simply to acknowledge that our justification lies in Jesus Christ's death, resurrection, and inevitable return and not in the satisfaction we momentarily feel.[5]

The hope and waiting that sanctifies our exploration frees us to treat other people's questions as more important than our own. The burden becomes clearest once people begin leading discussions. When I first made the shift from participant to leader, I thought that leading a discussion would be similar to having one. I quickly discovered that to lead well, I needed to set aside my own insights and interests in the text for the sake of my students, who were not yet able to think on the same level as I did. Similarly, to tell them the insights would have been to rob them of the work and thereby the growth and joy of reaching them on their own. And when people who have toiled and worked, have struggled and fought, finally catch a glimpse of that which they have longed for—there is enough joy there to make us forget ourselves altogether. The sacrifice of our own interests required of those who lead discussions, though, is simply that which we all ought pursue to cultivate the virtues we need to question well.

LEARNING THE QUESTIONS OF THE PAST

"Teach me not," T. S. Eliot writes in *The Four Quartets*, "of the wisdom of the past, but of their failures."[6] I might add "their

---

5. But we should avoid the self-consciousness of the public martyr's mindset, please, lest we have our reward in full.

6. Eliot, *Four Quartets*.

questions," too. The moment each new generation awakes and discovers itself in a strange world, they face the temptation to believe that they are the first to reach an undiscovered country, especially if the church has neglected to hand down a tradition to them. But a properly traditioned community passes down both the tenets of the faith and the questions that accompany them.[7] When the questions are forgotten, tradition ossifies into a rigid, hardened legalism that everyone must accept even if no one can remember why.

Something like this goes on in Jesus' day with respect to Sabbath observance. In Mark 2, Jesus' disciples pick grain on the Sabbath, which the Pharisees viewed as breaking the commandment. But Jesus goes behind the Law to the structure of creation in His response: "The Sabbath was made for man, not man for the Sabbath."[8] For all their observance, the Pharisees had forgotten the more fundamental question to which "Remember the Sabbath day" was the answer.

Legalism is still in our midst, but the greater intellectual danger is from a more rampant reduction of the faith to banal clichés. "Let go and let God." "God will work it out." "It's a God thing." "Everything happens for a reason." "It is what it is." And a thousand others. Every community has its own, even if we are frequently oblivious to them. Clichés may have meant something once, but once they are disconnected from their context, they become fragments of a forgotten way of life.[9]

Clichés stop thought prematurely. They are a retreat from the hazards of thinking; we run from the unknown into the

---

7. Catechisms get close to this, but robust teaching in church history and the development of doctrine would help a great deal as well.

8. Mark 2:27 (ESV).

9. See: Fred Sanders, *The Deep Things of God: How the Trinity Changes Everything* (Wheaton: Crossway Books, 2010).

comfortability of platitudes. And as preemptive efforts to close off our inquiries, they tend to undermine our desire for understanding the moment they are uttered.

One of my "favorite" clichés is that we "shouldn't put God in a box." That may be true on one level. But what if God has put Himself in a box, like a Scripture-shaped box? What then? Is the problem the box or the shape? If it was a circle-box that were infinitely large, could God fit inside of it? What if we have to be able to say *this* and *not that* of something in order to know it? If we say "God doesn't judge," does that put God in a box? (Yes, I just dropped one cliché against the other.) If God isn't in a box, even a Jesus-shaped box, can we know Him? Does God know He lacks a box? Is He able to communicate to His creatures the shape of a box He could fit in? I think the cliché means something like "God is ineffable," a beautiful word that simply means "beyond speech." But does God have a language for His own ineffability? Can He teach it to us?

That is a barrage of questions, I realize, but they come like a flood every time I hear someone say not to "put God in a box." I don't know the answers, but I do know that the cliché short-circuits the process of finding them. The cliché is of the soul-shrinking, mind-denying variety.

It is the nature of clichés to avoid examination. That is how they end up as clichés, because they are uttered with the authority of "Everyone knows that . . ." regardless of whether anyone knows *that* at all. They are platitudinous precisely because we think they are beyond question. But those who question well recognize that what everyone treats as obvious often isn't. When Jesus meets a lame man at the pool of Bethesda, He asks whether the man wants to be healed. It's a funny question that most of us would never ask. *Of course* people who are lame want to be healed.

But where we make assumptions, Jesus poses a question. Resisting the urge to resort to clichés would be a good start for any community to begin questioning well.

THE COUNTERREACTION AGAINST CLICHÉS

Communities that prematurely close down questions produce reactionary questioners. A faith that is not oriented toward understanding is a faith in name only. And if a community shows no interest in understanding the revelation that it purports to follow, then its children will react accordingly. When communities are reduced to repeating clichés, those with eager intellects who are raised in those communities will want to ask questions but have no sense of questioning well. We know there is something vital missing. But reactions can quickly become overreactions, as when a teetotaler first takes up drink. Or like Shakespeare's monkish Angelo in *Measure for Measure*, whose repressed sexual desires run rampant after years of being dormant. If people do not learn to question well, then they will almost certainly question badly.

I've seen young people who have never spent much time in an environment where they are free to ask questions overreact and run about questioning everything, all the time, always for an initial season. I may have even done that myself.[10] When I taught high school, it was not uncommon for parents to remark about how their newly invigorated students had started dominating the dinnertime conversation by raising questions about, well, everything.

We should welcome young people's budding questions and inquiries as signs of life and desire, not apostasy. We send our young people off to college presumably so they can become reflective, critical thinkers about the world around them. Yet the decision couldn't be more ironic, as it's just those virtues of the

---

10. May have. The memory, you know, goes quickly now that I am getting older.

intellectual life that we have often crowded out of our church communities. [11] By outsourcing the task of intellectual formation to colleges and universities, churches rob their young people of the very tools they need to think Christianly in their academic pursuits. Hence the anxieties that have fueled so many Christian college preparation ministries, which have gamely attempted to step into this gap.

But we must do more than pay lip service to questioning well; within the church, questioning must be modeled, integrated into the lives of our saints so that those who are young, and young in the faith, can see what the sanctification of our exploration looks like. If people are given little by way of formation, then it is folly to expect much from them. And if we do not like the intellectual fruit our communities produce, then we would do well to begin by reexamining their vines.

On Dialogue and the Church

Christians have sometimes inhibited healthy questioning, no doubt. Some contemporary critics have identified certain community structures, including sermons and Sunday school, as inherently antithetical to good questions. They have mused about replacing these pillars of the church's teaching practices with a format more conducive to good inquiry: the back and forth of dialogues. Didacticism is out; dialectics are in. Rearrange the chairs in a circle, pass the scented candle, and let's get started.

The retrieval of dialogue has been one of the most humorous ironies of the so-called "emerging church." Dialogue isn't unique to the philosopher Plato, but it was certainly promoted heavily by

---

11. It is tempting to treat critical reflection as a sign of a critical heart. And the one may quickly and subconsciously become the other and so does not stand outside of scrutiny. Yet within many church communities, those who are willing to ask questions still feel like outsiders.

him. Which is funny because the very people trumpeting dialogue these days have also been among the loudest decrying the "Platonic" influences on early Christianity. Apparently, their denunciations gave them cover to smuggle his method in through the back door. Don't get me wrong: on the whole, I'm a fan of dialogue. But I've come square up against its limits. If I am a dialogue critic, it is only because I am first and foremost a dialogue fan and because the limits we place around it are essential for its flourishing.

It is one of the misfortunes of our era that churches that emphasize dialogue have soured the method by disconnecting it from the sharp edges of creedal affirmations and proclamation from the pulpit. The result is that for many evangelicals, "dialogue" has become little more than a punch line. But we should be methodological pluralists. Dialogue is buttressed and made healthy when we submit ourselves to the authoritative pronouncement of the gospel by qualified ministers. And where the gospel takes root, it fosters a love of understanding—a love that takes the form of inquiry and questioning within a communal context. The public proclamation that Christ is King can and must coexist with a communal disposition to inquire and consider the meaning of that kingship.[12] If there is a dichotomy between dialogue and didactics, it cannot survive for long.

The appropriate integration of questioning into the church can only begin with leadership that is so committed to the truth of God's revelation that it fosters inquiry about it—and about their interpretations of it. A questioning community helps authorities avoid becoming authoritarian, for it reminds us of the gap between our interpretation of the infallible Word and the infal-

---

12. One way my own church home for five years in St. Louis, The Journey, did this was by providing a moderated, closed online forum for church attendees to discuss their questions with each other and with the church leadership. An experiment, it has proved (by and large) successful.

libility of that Word. The question of *what this text says* is not the same as *whether this text is inerrant or inspired*. It is no infringement on the infallible, inspired, authoritative Word of God to inquire about our pastor's interpretations of it.

If anything, communities that love authority the most will question best, for they will demonstrate a deeper love for the truth on which any authority must ultimately and finally be based. Belief in the authority of Scripture or of those who expound it doesn't end our exploration. It invigorates it by guiding it. We look to our pastor's and church's proclamations for guidance and for insight into the meaning of the text. We give authorities the "benefit of the doubt." Their training, expertise, and familiarity with the text means that we should privilege their interpretation above our own. But when we inquire, we search through the text after them to try to see things as they do. We read what they read and look along with them. Pastors who don't "show their exegetical work" in their sermons should be especially open to and encouraging of their flock's questions.

Within the church, elders and the body have distinct responsibilities. We are commanded to avoid "foolish, ignorant controversies" that "breed quarrels." And elders are responsible for preserving "sound doctrine," which means exercising oversight. But those responsibilities mean even more that pastors should willingly submit themselves to questioning and that they should model healthy inquiry themselves. As authoritative voices within the community, they should be first to establish such a deep humility before the truth that they are constantly deepening their knowledge of it. Where people are not free to question their leaders, those who are disposed to question will do so to excess. And it is not a sign of weakness when leaders submit themselves and their decisions to be questioned publicly but a sign of their confidence and desire for integrity.[13] For the authority of pastors and leaders of the church is not absolute, nor should they ever present it that way. It is derived and exists to the extent that their teaching corresponds to the revealed Word of God.[14]

WELCOMING THE DOUBTING

Can our churches feel like home to those who feel homeless? There will always be some people who don't understand the displacement that questioning can result in, who can't relate to how the intellectual journey sometimes feels like trudging through the wilderness. Faith has a variety of forms. It is the human dimension of our salvation, available to all. But it is also one of the "spiritual gifts" given to the church.[15] Within the body of Christ, some will be called to manifest their faith more deeply and clearly for the benefit and edification of others—and some may be so called to live out their questions in the same way. To each is given according to the measure of his faith. But we are one body, all working together for the glory of God in Christ. Still, it can be hard for those whose questions morph into doubts to find room within the church. The hesitating moments of uncertainty—the first half of all those psalms—rarely show up in our worship liturgies. Many churches have taken it upon themselves to disciple us in joy. But they have not taught us the mourning, and in moments when sin and brokenness come upon us, we do not know how to respond.

---

13. Two terms to note: by "questioned" I mean more than "being asked for advice." I include within this those who raise uncertainties about decisions or interpretations. And by "confidence," I mean that confidence that is rooted in the trustworthiness of Scripture's veracity and not their own need to always be right.

14. I recognize that there are considerable difficulties involved in identifying precisely when this is, and I do not wish to brush by them. My point is that authoritative teaching within the church leaves that question open for inquiry, such that we should all adopt the posture of the Bereans who search out the Scriptures to discern whether the teaching we hear indeed does correspond. See Acts 17:11.

15. 1 Corinthians 12:9 (ESV).

Similarly, the (appropriate) emphasis on faith often forgets to ac-knowledge the possibility of faith's frailty. When that occurs, our proclamations about faith take the tone of expectation and law rather than of exhortation toward a deeper and more assured con-fidence and maturity. When we forget that we were once weak, we quickly demand that everyone be strong.

It is a perennial temptation for who see to say to the doubting, "Come. I will show you the way." And sometimes, that is precisely what those who are consumed with their questions need. There is always a danger that those who doubt will integrate the posture into their self-understanding in ways that undermine the possibil-ity of escape, particularly if we make our doubts public and they draw a crowd.[16] We learn to enjoy the emotional struggle, the tur-moil, the upheaval that sometimes accompanies uncertainty. And we should not forget the lesson from Jesus and the paraplegic: not all who are doubting want to let their divided mind go in order to enter into the confidence of faith. We can pose a question to those who doubt about whether they want to believe or not. Having mercy on those who doubt does not entail demanding that they leave their condition if they have no desire to. Still, given the dif-ficulties in discernment, we should err on the side of waiting with each other and pointing toward the finality of heaven, retelling to each other the narrative of grace and the freedom and forgive-ness of our sins. For those who wish to be strong and believe may spend years striving to enter the healing waters before Jesus

---

16. I should note here an important difference, which Brian Auten helped me clarify: I speak of the sort of existential doubts that we have about the truthfulness of Christianity. In situations where a church's leadership is abusive or harmful, then there is a time and place for "going public" (by which we almost always mean writing online) with concerns if they are not addressed properly through other means. The question of doubting church leadership is a distinct one, it seems to me, from those doubts I am pursuing here—though it is easy to see how a bad experience with the former might lead one to doubt Christianity's truthfulness altogether.

comes and lifts them in.

Fostering self-critical inquiry is particularly difficult for the church, given that our faith is public and that it has boundaries. We publicly enter the church through baptism. And that membership means affirming the articles of faith and moral codes that set the criteria for full membership in the community. We are a people who point to the risen Christ and say, *This one, He is Lord.* Such a witness means specification and distinction, difference and otherness, from those who do not share our confession. The uniqueness of such a community is presumed in the granting of authority to the disciples in Matthew 18:18 and is reaffirmed in its own way in 1 Corinthians 5:1-3. We proclaim one Lord, one faith, one baptism—which means dissension and rabble rousing are not abstract possibilities but genuine threats to the church's authoritative witness to the life of Jesus.[17] The formal, institutional unity we strive for shapes our intellectual lives as well. Affirming such boundaries does not foreclose the possibility of an "honest conversation" about them—another cliché that needs to go. But it does establish a frame for the church's communal life and witness to the world.

Making our questioning and doubts known in such an environment can be difficult, which is why those who inquire may need a good deal of courage. Many people simply won't understand the struggle that long-suffering and waiting for answers often means, even (and especially!) for those inquiries that are made reverently, soberly, and in the fear of God. And the likelihood of being misinterpreted is very high. The differences between questions seeking understanding and those seeking to undermine are sometimes imperceptible and can only be known upon reflection and upon their fruit.

---

17. How churches should interact with bloggers is a book of its own. But I will not be writing it.

Yet when questions come upon us, we must wrestle with them and sometimes wrestle publicly, remembering always the admonitions about not scandalizing those who may be weak in the faith. The criteria of making our questions public should always be edifying and strengthening the faith and charity of those we live with—even if that means allowing them the courtesy of carrying our burdens with us. We do well to bring our searching and exploring under wise and authoritative pastoral counsel, especially when making the decision to broadcast them beyond the confines of our local communities and to the world beyond.

Such counsel is particularly important when our exploring leads us to question realms that churches accept as givens, as the possibility for controversy and misunderstanding increases. I have sometimes gotten myself in trouble for questioning things that other people take for granted. To choose one recent example, I proposed that the church's public witness should *sometimes* involve silence on matters of significant controversy, even when we have a real interest and concern. My piece was posted in the middle of an uproar about the politics of marriage and it did not go over well. I try to treat my stances on those questions with a very open hand. The question of when and how we speak in defense of our positions isn't core to the faith; it's a matter of interpretative fidelity and public prudence. And so my proposal is revisable.[18] Yet many people whom I admire misunderstood my position and responded with surprising hostility. By calling into question a particular mode

---

18. I doubtlessly did not communicate this well within the piece itself or the venue where I posted it. Both of which make the reaction more understandable. But sometimes inquiry and questioning take a different form than adding question marks at the end. Sometimes exploration happens by way of floating hypothesis as "trial balloons," as it were, to see how they go over. I think a good deal more openness to revision would help temper our public discourse in healthy ways.

of operating, I ran aground of a taboo.[19] And my own lack of prudence in raising my concerns caused needless scandal.

The home the church provides to the intellectually homeless
comes furnished, which can be something of a scandal to those of
us disposed to want to question world without end. When we
enter this community, we yield ourselves and allow our desires to
be discipled and redirected. The cry of affirmation that marks our
entry—"I believe"—may be provisional. It may be stammering and
tentative. It may be accompanied by the pleading "Help my unbelief." But our churches are not blank canvases wherein people of
all types can gather to be left alone: as a community of love, centered on the revelation of Jesus, the church has an authoritative
witness with a shape that graciously forms the beliefs of those
who are her members.

In proclaiming the good news of Christ's death and resurrection, the church reminds those who question that the negative
spaces we feel so keenly are full of the radiating glory of God.
The church provides a reminder that the felt absence of God is a
temporary moment to teach us to look for the resurrection of the
dead and the life of the world to come. As the church schools us
in prayer, our interrogatives become one part of the symphony of
our speech. We learn to orient our questioning around our proper
interlocutor, God Himself.

Which is to say, the church welcomes those of us with fears
and doubts without hesitation and without—question. But like
the gentle nurse to the moribund hospital patient, she also under-
takes for us the slow and painful work of diagnosing our ailments
and providing us relief.

---

19. I do not regret the decision to post the piece, even while I wish I had made my
position clearer than I did initially. One thing I realized is that when taboos get
called into question, people often have little patience for the back-and-forth of a
dialogue or for subsequent explanation of our views.

QUESTIONING, COURAGE, AND GRACE—FOR THE CHURCH

The paradox is that those who doubt often need to extend the very mercy they need to receive. It's not easy for churches to know how to handle those who are in the travails of doubt. Those who sit with divided souls must be willing to colabor, to fellowship in another's sufferings, to bear another's burden to keep up their strength. And the church often fails at that. It might seem problematic that a church that proclaims mercy would struggle to extend it. But what else would we expect, given that the church is made up of humans living in a fallen world, awaiting its final perfection? Each time those who doubt are failed by the church, they will be drawn one step deeper into maturity if they extend grace to those who have given none.

It is partly for this reason that we should not give up meeting together, even if we are wracked with doubt. If we remove ourselves from the context of prayer, worship, and the proclamation of the Word, then we cut ourselves off from the very mysterious, secret formation of our hearts and minds that helps us escape our doubts. Continuing to attend may feel like suffering. But if Karl Barth is right, then "suffering and not triumph" is just what the church means.[20] The church is sometimes the place where we feel the sufferings of Christ on the cross the most.

I'd even go one step further: When those who doubt or question orient their lives toward the edification of the body of Christ, the very frailties and problems that they feel become gifts and signs of the church's witness. The church welcomes those who doubt not as object lessons of what to avoid but as signs of God's grace and reminders of the frailty of belief in a fallen world. As

---

20. Karl Barth, *The Epistle to the Romans* Edwyn Clement Hoskyns (London: Oxford University Press, H. Milford, 1933), 334.

the church listens and attends to those who struggle, its exhortation to believe will be more insistent, more urgent and powerful. What's more, those who feel the absences and endure until the end reorient the church's witness away from the immediate satisfaction of emotional lives toward faithful obedience regardless of the circumstances.

None of this means that doubt or questioning are grounds for boasting—may it never be! If anything, when we orient our lives toward the edification of others, we begin to see the ways in which our lives are entangled in the very mindsets that aggravated us—we catch glimpses of the planks firmly lodged in our eyes. It is tempting for those of us who question to be frustrated at other people's "naïve belief" and their simplistic acceptance of authority. Yet we too believe all sorts of things on authority, without questioning—and quite reasonably so. None of us has done the experiments demonstrating that light acts simultaneously like a wave and particles. Yet broad-minded, reasonable people that we want to be, we are happy to accept it.[21]

Nor can we allow the experience of marginalization within the church to sour into bitterness and recrimination. I understand the frustrated dismissals of anti-intellectualism and the tacit, unstated hostility toward critical thinking. I have at various points in my life sounded all those complaints and then some.[22] Jokes about seminarians are still acceptable in places that otherwise value the intellectual dimension of the Christian life. But as long as our inquiry is

---

21. The sort of claims we should accept from the sciences and the reasons for those claims is, of course, a major question for Christians. My point here is simply that accepting claims on authority is not limited to Christians who believe in revelation.

22. And I have even had the temerity to direct some of those objections against the so-called young evangelicals. See my piece "The New Evangelical Scandal," in *The City* (winter 2008). Available online at http://www.civitate.org/2009/01/the-new-evangelical-scandal/.

rooted in the love of Jesus and His church, then we who question should cultivate compassion for those who do not. If a life of inquiry is part of a flourishing life and community, then the first response for those who reject it must be prayer and intercession.

Similarly, it is important for those of us who are questioning to remember that our exploration into the unknown is only one facet of our following in the way of Jesus. When questions and doubts come upon us, they have a way of skewing our perspective on the world. In severe cases, they can paralyze us from making decisions or serving our neighbors. But as long as we continue to care for the orphans and widows, then the broader context of our lives with Christ will keep our inquiries in their appropriate context—as important moments in our pursuit of understanding, but by no means the sum of the Christian life. The moment our questions stand in the way of our loving and serving our neighbors is the moment we must lay them down.

Can the church be a place where we can ask our questions, and even a place where those afflicted by doubts can feel the welcome safety of a home? It often will not feel like it, for the home that we enter into is one that demands our death. There is no place so dangerous to our existence, no place that demands so much as the place where Christ is proclaimed as King. For in taking on Christ's life as ours, we find our own lives and pursuits laid down on behalf of others. Our searching and exploring, our doubting and our weakness, these too are given to us not only for our own good and God's glory but for the building up of the people of God. We travel by faith, each with the measure we have been apportioned and with the degree of confidence that God has granted us. For the church is a wounded but merry band, walking together arm in arm down the long road toward that final day when all the songs we sing now shall be swept up into the great chorus of Hallelujahs and Amens.

8

Friendship, Disagreement, and
Our Fundamental Commitments

> *What loneliness is more lonely than distrust?*
> —GEORGE ELIOT[1]

"There are two kinds of people in this world," my friend and Oxford professor remarked in the midst of a rollicking argument about the church. He, more liberal than I and a devout Anglican, wanted the church to relinquish some of its historical positions to keep the tent as broad as possible. I sounded my disagreement and we plodded our way through the problems. The conversation was spirited but respectful, as all such disagreements ought to be.

"And what kinds are those?" I took the bait. Anytime someone establishes a stark dichotomy like that, there's an obligation to play along.

"Uniters and dividers," he said. "And I am a uniter."

There aren't many moments when I have a halfway witty

---

1. George Eliot, *Middlemarch* (London: W. Blackwood and Sons, 1901), 318.

comeback waiting, but this was one.

"Indeed. And I'm with Jesus and His sword, which turns son against father and brother against brother." Point scored, he granted, and we moved on.

Because I write about controversial issues, I often find myself in the company of individuals whose presence I thoroughly enjoy, even when I disagree with them. Our conversations are often similar to the one I had with my professor: while we aren't bashful about trying to persuade each other, we find ourselves surprised by what we agree upon even as we find more interesting ways to disagree. It's not a happy-touchy-feely-let's-just-get-along approach, or even an approach that is willing to rest content with understanding each other. We value the friendship not because of the disagreements *per se* but because of the goods that emerge through them.

Like my good friend Tyler Wigg Stevenson. Tyler is one of the most thoughtful people I know. As the founder of the Two Futures Project, Tyler has spent a lot of time working to rid the world of nuclear weapons. Our disagreements on those questions and others are subtle but very real. Yet my friendship with him goes beyond our differences: as we have spent time talking, I have gotten to know him and have seen his many virtues. I rarely leave a conversation without something new to consider. My respect for him is nearly boundless—which is why I do him the courtesy of disagreeing with him in the most vigorous way possible when necessary. But it's the goods of friendship that make such conversations genuinely worthwhile.

"Opposition is true friendship,"[2] William Blake wrote, a phrase that C. S. Lewis would later use in reference to his friend

---

2. William Blake, *The Marriage of Heaven and Hell* (Mineola, NY: Courier Dover Publications, 1994), 40.

and sparring partner Owen Barfield. But it was G. K. Chesterton and George Bernard Shaw who may be the best twentieth-century examples. The two had nearly diametrically opposed philoso-phies, were both enormously clever—and in Chesterton's case, simply enormous—yet became very good friends through a series of lively public debates that they held around England.[3] In fact, when their debates ended, their friendship waned. Though both expressed a desire to see more of each other, their paths rarely crossed.

Aristotle might have been overstating things when he noted that friends have all things in common, but he was right that there has to be *some* ground on which two people can meet as peers. Friendship can survive opposition only as long as the friends share other goods. When two people inquire together—when they won-der, What *is* true about the world?—their common pursuit forms a "common ground," even if the answers each person puts forward are fundamentally different. And the paradox is that in that ex-ploration we not only learn more about the world but also about the character and virtues of those who survey its terrain in their pursuit of truth and understanding. Inquiry doesn't simply happen between friends, that is. It can make us friends as well.

Switching the Spectrum

When my wife and I got married, I would sometimes joke that while other folks were "one flesh" people, I was a "twoness" guy. I am well acquainted with the biblical language about the marital union and heartily endorse it, properly understood. But my wife and I determined not to have the unity candle at our wedding because the joining has to leave us intact as individual persons. There's something chilling about seeing the side candles

---

3. And all the Chesterton fans nodded. (And knew this joke was coming.)

extinguished, leaving only the solitary flame representing the now unified couple.

My wife is the most intelligent woman I know and the clearest thinker, too. Her perceptiveness is an incredible gift but has also been the source of a good deal of humorous frustration. I have strong intuitions about the world, the reasons for which are often imperceptible to me when I first set out to explain myself. I have to do a good deal of exploring even to find the grounds for my own stances. That can be frustrating for my wife, as it can take me a good deal of trial and error to get my arguments out with the sort of clarity and precision she prefers.

Those temperamental differences make life interesting, though. While I am occasionally tempted to overcome them, they serve as a constant reminder that she and I are not the same. And if every difference were to go, then love would disappear with them. The Godhead is perfectly united as the (individuated) Father, Son, and the Spirit—which is *the* mystery at the center of reality. As long as God remains Himself in Himself, He also remains distinct within Himself—and so is love.

Disagreement is even more of a struggle, though, when people don't share the same fundamental commitments about the world. My wife and I both love Jesus. We both are striving to know Him better. Things aren't quite so straightforward with John Corvino, who is a gay atheist apologist—or at the other end of the "spectrum" of everything I believe. John is extremely bright, level-headed, and fair. And fun to hang out with. He is someone for whom I have a great deal of respect. His concern for others, his honesty, and his commitment to discovering the truth leave space for genuine friendship, despite the serious gaps between our outlooks.

To say that we are at opposite ends of the "spectrum" is a

bit deceptive, though. While many of our fundamental commit-ments are very different, we have others in common. Switch up the "spectrum" and John and I would be on the same side of it. We both care about making good arguments, for instance, even when it means disagreeing with others who share our conclusions.[4] We both care about speaking reasonably and care about understand-ing those we disagree with. And we care that our conceptions of the world ultimately prove true. From those standpoints, we have a good deal more in common than not.

Such common pursuits provide the context for a friendship, despite our significant opposition to each other's intellectual posi-tions. We both think we have the truth.[5] But when we enter into the exchange of reasons, we don't presume that we've understood the other straightaway but explore the world by considering it through each other's frameworks. We listen and understand and then enter into our critiques.

As I've already mentioned, inquiring creates a momentary gap between beliefs and the person. A person's life may be shaped by how they see the world, but it cannot be reduced to it. Our com-mitments are not objects; they form us and our lives form them. But in the moment of inquiry, we distance ourselves from them as we consider them. That process of consciously explaining and clarifying our framework necessarily distances us from our self-understanding—otherwise who or what is doing the explaining or clarifying?[6] To be suspended there permanently is impossible. But in feeling it for a moment, we can also recognize that the per-son goes beneath and beyond their outlook—the image of God is

---

4. And even while I struggle to adduce my reasons for my intuitions, I think it's a critically important process.

5. Of course. While we're open to being wrong, if we knew that we were wrong, we'd change our beliefs.

6. If one person is not inquiring and so sees no gap between their beliefs and their person—then the problem will endure.

never extinguished, despite our sins and errors. That recognition on both sides means that disagreement can happen without it resulting in or leading to the rejection of the person.

But John and I also try not to presume we have nothing more to learn from each other. Even though we think our perspectives are true, we don't foreclose on the possibility we might have taken a wrong turn somewhere. And that means we occasionally come up against questions neither of us can answer. There's more in the world than is dreamt of in our philosophies (and theology!), and that means inquiring together as much as it does attempting to persuade each other. Our shared love of truth means that when we bump up against the unknown, a negative space, we both want to inquire about its shape and see if we might discover something we hadn't seen before.

A posture of inquiry and exploration allows us to question *along with* others, even those whose commitments don't match our own. Such a posture means not determining beforehand what we will discover when we set out. We both will have our orthodoxies, which are going to shape what we see. But the joy of inquiry is that we may just find ourselves surprised, either with more understanding of the world than we had before or with new beliefs that have replaced false ones. If we rule out either as possibilities, then we stand in danger of replacing a genuine conversation with the mutual repetition of talking points.

FOUNDATIONAL COMMITMENTS AND THE POSSIBILITY OF INQUIRY

How can we consider fairly and honestly perspectives with which we disagree? Given how rarely we see people do so publicly, it is apparently quite a challenge. We live in echo chambers, which repeat slogans and clichés while reacting with suspicion to claims that come from the "other side." Our public dialogues are rife with a rank polarization, where the disagreements run so deep that conversations across party lines that don't start with defense and critique are taken as a betrayal of principles.

We might hope that Christians would point toward a more excellent way of dialoguing, but (alas) we often do not. Throw in the added layer of sanctification, and disagreements stand in danger of being reduced to a referendum on everyone's holiness.[7] To raise a point of disagreement in the church (or within the broader Christian Internet community) is to hazard being accused of dissension and divisiveness, of engaging in needless quarrels and controversies. The church gathers around shared beliefs and the practices that sustain them. Anyone is welcome to watch, but certain aspects of the church's life are closed to those who do not affirm her creed. We are a people under authority, and I will be the first to admit it and abide by it. But the desire to preserve the role of authority within the church has been hardened in light of the (perceived) pressures from those who wished to replace authoritative teaching and practices with an open-ended conversation. As such, a healthy authority is in constant danger of degenerating into authoritarian closed-mindedness, which reduces all disagreement to dissension rather than patiently abiding it out of the unshakable confidence that truth will prevail.[8]

It is true, of course, that some questions are veiled attacks.

---

7. The amount of throat-clearing about how much we love the other guy before going on to say why he's absolutely, abysmally wrong would be humorous if it wasn't tedious. And good luck getting those on the "same side" to bring up their disagreements publicly. That's apparently not what people on the same team do. There is a time and place for a unified witness and message. But the reluctance to disagree with our friends publicly actually seems more like a sign of our frailty, not maturity, as though demonstrating any sort of internal disagreement would threaten to bring the house of cards down.

8. I am in no way suggesting that there are no wolves among the sheep—only that those who question are not necessarily among them.

But all are not. Unfortunately, leaders who have not learned to question well will struggle to tell the difference and so tend to lump them all under the same antiauthoritarian banner. When questions come from people within the church, the leaders should be predisposed to welcome and encourage them. Questioning will tend to be subversive in communities where questioning is not practiced. When inquiry is modeled and discipled, the gap between healthy questioning and subversive questioning will be easier to discern. I have long wondered—and the question is unanswerable—whether Adam and Eve might have been better prepared to see and reject the serpent's game if they had inquired themselves before they learned to question from the serpent. We should not underestimate the expulsive power of healthy questioning, in other words. For it is not whether we will inquire but only when and how.

Yet how should we respond when people begin doubting foundational commitments, rather than important incidentals? Whether the shape of the gospel, the authority of revelation, the status of a fetus, the nature of truth, or the meaning of sexuality, differences on such core positions often generate very different ways of thinking and acting in the world.[9] Many of the sharpest divisions in the church can be traced back to these questions.

When such disagreements happen, providing reasons for our positions proves incredibly difficult. Our foundational commitments are often givens for us—we work outward from them, rather than the other way around. As a result, they often function as boundary markers, which give the community that holds them its distinctive character. Controversy lurks the moment they are dug up and called into question. When the foundations are shaken,

---

9. Of course, what is a foundational commitment in one community may not be in another. And while some issues may seem like surface issues, the differences may hinge on other, deeper differences that are closer to differences over first principles.

people man the defenses.[10]

And for good reason. Sometimes defense is precisely what is called for. As Chesterton pointed out, there are thoughts that stop thought—and they merit satire and a healthy dose of scorn. When the gospel was threatened in Galatia, Paul responded with thunderous rebukes. When Jesus denounced opponents with "woes," He humorously added the lawyers to His list after one of them piped up because he was offended.[11] There's a lot of room within the Christian witness for sharp lines, sharp words, and sharp disagreements. My friend Tyler and I don't hold back our rhetoric about each other's positions, in part because we know how much depends on them. Respect, love, and care for the other have fueled our disputes as much as they have moderated them.

Yet there are stark differences between the world of Jesus and Paul and our own. Neither of them were cloistered within an echo chamber, as we tend to be these days. Paul listened closely enough to the best philosophy of his day to take his message to Mars Hill. Jesus offered His above pronouncements in the company of those at whom He aimed them and suffered their responses. When Jesus warns His followers to beware the teaching of the Pharisees, He exhorts them to "watch" it, not ignore it altogether.[12] The paradox is that as information has become more widely available, our worlds have become more narrow. We tend to have our approved list of people that we read and listen to and anyone not on that list (or not recommended by it) is treated with suspicion. We live in intellectual enclaves, where we hear and regurgitate that which we

---

10. Sometimes, the controversy erupts not due to those who are genuinely questioning but from those who have previously rejected those first principles and then make their objections known. I would argue that under such circumstances, we ought still begin with a posture of open inquiry given that others observing the exchange may be somewhere in the middle.

11. Luke 11:45–46 (ESV). I owe this point to Doug Wilson.

12. Matthew 16:6 (ESV).

were already disposed to accept and rarely have our presuppositions challenged. [13]

In such an environment, the sort of polemical denouncements that Jesus and Paul practiced entertain the faithful but do little else. We examine and test others out of our fervent desire to defend the truth. But we are a good deal less eager to "Examine [ourselves], to see whether [we] are in the faith," as Paul exhorts the Corinthians, either institutionally or individually. [14] Self-criticism in movements is a sign of health and confidence, when it is undertaken with a desire to understand and grow. And cultivating a posture of self-criticism helps protect our thunderous denouncements uttered with the tongues of angels from sounding like tinny dismissals coming from clanging gongs.

We need a polemics and defense that is aimed first at restoration rather than separation. As a people who proclaim "one Lord, one faith, one baptism," the unity of the church is as much a witness to the world as our truthful proclamation. Unity is an article of faith, which means it is sometimes affirmed despite appearances rather than because of them. But it is still on us to cultivate and preserve unity inasmuch as we can. Holding out the hope of reconciliation to those who call into question our foundational commitments is just as important as delineating the truth. Paul even pursues the sharp judgment of a gross moral failure in 1 Corinthians 5 "so that [the offender's] spirit may be saved in the day of the Lord." [15] It is a judgment that Paul can render precisely because he recognizes that his authority is bound by the truth, that it is an authority that is "for building up and not for tearing down," and

---

13. One of the most haunting and accurate descriptions that I know of the "enclave society" is Jeffrey Stout's. See Jeffrey Stout, *Democracy and Tradition* (Princeton, NJ: Princeton University Press, 2004), 114.

14. 2 Corinthians 13:5 (ESV).

15. 1 Corinthians 5:5 (ESV).

that it is encompassed by his prayers for the Corinthian church.[16] If we genuinely felt the weight of judgment, labored in prayer for others, and mourned the tragedy of the task before us, I suspect we might be less hasty to draw lines and a good deal more effective when we did so.

One way to aim for restoration with those who are wandering is to set about questioning alongside them. This may mean momentarily opening our own central commitments. But the more confidence we have in the truthfulness of our own framework, the easier it will be to inquire about whether it is true.[17] Like all virtues, confidence has its false and distorted approximations. And one of its cheapest is a reactionary and hand-wringing defensiveness that passes itself off as rallying around the truth. To twist around a Teddy Roosevelt line, those who are truly confident will be able to speak softly and question more patiently precisely because they have at their disposal a hefty intellectual stick.[18]

The paradox, though, is that if we respond to the rejection, doubting, or questioning of Christianity's core commitments by maintaining our resolve to seek understanding, we shall find ourselves with more understanding. While our instinctive reaction may be to defend and retreat to ways of speaking that are comfortable and acceptable to us, if we momentarily set those responses aside and enter into rethinking the world in light of the question, we will find ourselves a good deal better off than we were at the start.

When foundational commitments become matters of controversy, they need some sort of justification. We cannot simply

---

16. This hope of reconciliation does not mean Christians should never pronounce ideas "anathema" or even acknowledge when people's beliefs have become heretical. The verse the quote is taken from is 2 Corinthians 13:10.

17. A process, I've pointed out elsewhere, that also engenders new ways of understanding than forgoing it altogether.

18. Whether we do this will depend on a host of factors, including the proximity of our relationship with the other person.

point at them and hope that people will accept them, even if we had been once able to. As theologian Robert Spaemann put it, "Even axiomatic beliefs need justifying in the long run if they face a challenge."[19] We must provide an account, in other words, re-articulating the world in such a way that the foundational commitments make sense. To use a recent example, when people question classical Christian teachings on sexuality, we can retreat and insist that "the Bible says so."[20] And the Bible may indeed "say so," and that may suffice as an explanation. Yet if we wish to seek understanding, we might put a question to it: "Why does the Bible say so?" The faith that seeks understanding has limits, but it ought not rest too early either. And presumably the Bible "says so" because it is *true*, which means we can find reasons beyond the Bible for our positions as well.

To put it differently, the more we live within the story and logic of Scripture, the more resources we will have to explain its internal reasons in ways that make them more plausible to others—even if others aren't immediately persuaded. As we live inside the story of Scripture, we will start to *see the point*. Its teachings will make sense of the world and the world will make sense of its teachings, enabling us to expand our use of resources so we can give a fully-orbed account of our positions. As Chesterton put it, "A man is not really convinced of a philosophic theory when he finds something that proves it. He is only really convinced when he finds that everything proves it."[21]

---

19. Robert Spaemann, *Persons: The Difference between "Someone" and "Something"* (New York: Oxford University Press, 2006), 3.

20. I choose this example because it is an obvious point of controversy that hinges on lots of other fundamental questions, like our understanding of the nature of the human person, the meaning of the body, the authority of Scripture, and the like. All these are tangled together, which makes traditional Christian teachings about sexuality feel like a fundamental, axiomatic commitment even if it isn't in the creed explicitly.

21. Chesterton, *Essential*, 56.

Entering into that sort of imaginative exploration of even our own foundational commitments will help us find new, fresh arguments and rhetoric to explain "the same old thing." As a friend once pointed out, the texts being used to demonstrate the divinity of Jesus are different today than in the early church. But the conclusions are the same. The tragic paradox is that if our instinctive reaction is defense, we may (ironically) cut ourselves off from the growth we need to rigorously defend our positions. Because if they are true, then there will be an abundance of reasons for them.

What's more, by reopening our commitments and being willing to inquire into them again, we will remind ourselves *why* we held those commitments in the first place. What hangs on Scripture's answer to this question? Why should we hold on to these positions? When we forget the answers to those questions, we will only be able to respond to questions by repeating what the Bible says while dismissing our neighbors as incapable of moral reasoning. Some people may be so incapable. But that is a judgment that we should conclude the conversation with, not begin it with, even when we start with the knowledge that they disagree with our core teachings. For such controversies are opportunities to demonstrate our intellectual long-suffering, to patiently and ploddingly continue pointing to the goods inherent within our position while unpacking them as persuasively as we can in a language others understand.

The Good of Intellectual Empathy

The ability to question alongside someone else is a form of "intellectual empathy." When we have it, we imaginatively enter into how another person is looking at the world. We go beyond the willing suspension of disbelief to momentarily granting premises and commitments that we might otherwise reject to see how their framework holds together—*if* the whole framework holds together—and to discern how to respond in light of that. Intellectual empathy is a form of seeing how. As in, "Oh, I see how you could think that. It's wrong, but I can see how it might make sense." Or as in, "Oh, I see how you're thinking there. That's wrong for the following seventeen reasons!" Or, "Yes, that *does* make sense. That's a good point." It is an act that is aimed first toward the good of understanding, a good that persuasion may flow from but can never precede.

Think about how we enjoy novels like *Lord of the Rings*. If we merely suspended judgment about the existence of hobbits, we might keep ourselves at a critical distance from the story but we wouldn't much enjoy it. We cannot empathize with characters if we keep reminding ourselves they do not exist. When we enter into a narrative, we imaginatively construct a world. The more consistent and detailed the world is, the easier it is to believe. *The Lord of the Rings* is one of the most successful novels ever because the depths to which Tolkien went to make up an integrated whole are without parallel.[22] Yet when the world doesn't make sense within its own terms, careful readers are able to detect that as well.

Like all virtues, intellectual empathy needs sharp edges to be of much use. In the same way that "compassion" can be reduced to a reactionary impulse that forgoes considering what is actually good for people, so too "mutual understanding" can be reduced to the goal of all our conversation, as though that is enough. And it is not. But we should not forgo the work of understanding, either, and skip straight to the verbal fireworks that come with objecting and denouncing.

Of course, intellectual empathy doesn't require giving up the foundational commitments that we have, any more than reading

---

22. A fact attested to by the oddish people who have learned Elvish.

The Lord of the Rings requires jettisoning our commitment to Jesus. It is precisely because of our confidence in the truthfulness of our own commitments that we are able to enter into how others see the world and have the freedom to explore along with them. As I argued previously, the more comfortable we are of where we are coming from, the more confident we will be in venturing out the door. And as Christians, given that God has already given us every square inch of the world before us, we can step out with the knowledge that all will be well.

I realize that having a posture of openness toward our foundational commitments sounds dangerous. And it is. My argument isn't that everyone should do it but that a well-ordered, mature Christian mind (and movement) will be capable of it. We won't always open up our core commitments. But when those around us do, we can step within their framework and find reasons within for why our own is more good, more true, and more beautiful.

Showing Our Work

I hated "showing my work" in math class. I could run numbers in my head and would often see the answers quickly. But that wasn't enough for my teachers; they wanted me to demonstrate my movement from question to answer, to make my thinking public, which was a process that I found tedious and redundant. I provided the right answer. Why wasn't that enough? One time it even got me into trouble: I noticed a more elegant solution to a math problem than the math teacher had taught us and so used it on my test. The next day I was up in front of the class, trying to teach other high schoolers who were totally uninterested. The humiliating episode reinforced my "geek" status and deepened my hatred of showing my work even more.

The problem, of course, is that beneath our "right answers"

there is a chain of reasoning that explains how we arrived at them. We may not remember that reasoning, and we may not have ever consciously deliberated our way through it. We may have grasped our understanding intuitively, without reflection. But when someone comes along and asks us, "Why?" we must reach down to the subterranean levels of thought and begin excavating.

I described the virtue of intellectual empathy above, but I might have used "hospitality" instead. I like to jokingly introduce my friend Tim King as a good friend who is "wrong about everything." He works for Sojourners and has opinions on poverty reduction that I think are problematic. Yet when we talk I take into my own mind his opinions and consider them from every angle, even when I know I don't agree with them. Or at least I try, anyway. Intellectual integrity takes us beyond having the truth or even being able to articulate it. It means having the courage to entertain—another hospitality word—the alternatives placed before us by those we respect and giving reasons when we discern they're wrong.[23] The only real danger is that I'm going to be convinced by Tim or better understand his stances for it.

In that process, though, we have to show our work. We ask "Why?" of each other, and then explain away. We give long lists of reasons for our positions (or sometimes, very short lists!) and those are evaluated and questioned to see whether they will stand up. In that mutual process of digging out our commitments and making public our chains of reasoning, we begin to grasp some of the subterranean issues that are often buried beneath the disagreements—our stories, personal experiences, and our worries and anxieties that have brought us to our differing conclusions.

But in that process we also make space for friendship. As Oliver O'Donovan has argued, beliefs are bound together: the

23. If they are wrong, that is.

isolated propositions that we encounter are only fragments of an interdependent system, a system that must be explored for the proposition to be appropriately understood.[24] When we look alongside someone at their frameworks and the commitments that take shape within them, we "begin to accompany [our interlocutor] as [we] challenge him and question him." We journey together, if only for a moment, and wonder how all these things can be.

The fruit of such intellectual empathy is persuasion. My goal is to convince Tim to see the world the way I do—and "doing unto others" means that I should open myself to the possibility of being converted by him. In my best moments, I don't want to win a debate for the sake of winning or for my own vanity. When we see the person beneath the arguments, we begin to be moved out of care and love *for the other*. I want Tim to change his opinions because he really is wrong and because I really care about him and being wrong really matters. And he approaches me the same way.

When we live in intellectual enclaves, persuasion ceases to be the point of our public discourse. In politics and the church, we have very little reasoning together and a good deal of repeating talking points and retreating to defend our positions. But friendships across party lines help us destroy caricatures. We find ourselves in conversations that reach down to the substantive disagreements, which is the place we must reach for genuine conversion to occur.

As Christians, we take an interest in the common good, the well-being of the society that we momentarily call home. But there can be no common good if there is no common ground. And if there is no intellectual empathy, no fundamental interest in understanding each other, there can be no space in which meaningful

---

24. A "system" that I have sometimes called a "framework," "outlook," or a "world." See Oliver O'Donovan's "Reflections on Pluralism" in *The Kuyper Center Review, Vol 1: Politics, Religion, and Sphere Sovereignty*, Gordon Graham, ed. (Grand Rapids, Eerdmans, 2010).

and *constructive* disagreement can occur. It is our calling and duty as the church to show the world a "more excellent way" in how we work out our intellectual disagreements and seek reconciliation with those who we think are leaving the faith behind. If the church is not willing to seek reconciliation within itself and frame its speech accordingly, then we deserve the polarized political environment that we currently decry.

In a sense, friendships with people who disagree take on a civic dimension. Me and Tim, *good for America*. It's a bit weird to think about a friendship on that broad of a scale (because even if it weren't good for America, I'd still enjoy his company). But it's true: friendships despite disagreement point toward a world where differences don't necessarily end relationships. These sorts of friendships that include the possibility of conversion and persuasion are one way we can play nicely as American citizens without compromising our Christian faith.[25]

Questioning Ourselves and the Good of Opposition

It's tempting to dismiss intellectual opposition altogether as problematic and seek to overcome it at any cost. Even if it were possible, it wouldn't be good. Opposition is an important source of intellectual and creative energy. Augustine and Athanasius wrote reams of content trying to disabuse the church of the heresies that had infiltrated it. Aquinas, Calvin, and Luther—all similarly giants—didn't shy away from a debate. Dante wrote beautiful poetry tossing his enemies into hell, Michelangelo painted his foes into it, and Solzhenitsyn wrote literature to end communism. My own intellectual hero, Chesterton, wrote a book called *Heretics*. A

---

25. I'm pretty sure even the Anabaptists would be on board with this. Also, this is a joke. Settle down, Anabaptists.

healthy dose of opposition clarifies what's at stake on an issue and sharpens our own thinking.

Yet the good opposition provides also come through questioning. A good question sets up an intellectual tension inside of us; it creates mental opposition to our own position. Is Jesus the eternally begotten Son of the Father? Seeking to understand the answer means considering the reasons why he might not be. It means momentarily thinking like a heretic in order to see why heretics are wrong—and why that particular wrong is so destructive and devastating. The question creates a pressure from which there must be a release, which is similar to the pressure created by the challenges posed by those who disagree with us.

The more we question ourselves, the more equipped we will be to interact with the questions of others. A question we have not encountered before can be disorienting. It can be humbling when we have to say that we don't know an answer. But when we work to understand our own beliefs by inquiring after them, we will cultivate the virtues that allow us to understand our friends' beliefs as well—and then interact with them appropriately. Understanding is a good that transcends creeds. And as Christians, it is the sort of good that we should pursue for others, as it is a good we want for ourselves. It's frustrating to have your position misunderstood, as everything that follows invariably misses the mark. To understand a position does not entail that we agree with it: but in a world marked by unsympathetic, hasty dismissals and cataclysmic, thunderous prognostications of doom, a strong dose of listening and considering might go a long way toward improving our discourse, both inside and outside the church.[26] We can train ourselves into such a posture by searching out and explor-

---

26. I have done all of these, I grant. But I work to make even my denunciations take the tone of "good news." But even when that doesn't happen, we should remember to occasionally keep the powder dry: if all we're doing is disagreeing and dismissing, then our voice will lose its force.

ing our own frameworks, by seeking to understand all we have already received.

The possibility for opposition isn't limited to major theological or moral questions, either. Whether our friends are Christians or not, whether they agree with our political stances or can't stand them, there will always be points of intellectual disagreement and opposition that emerge. When I was in college, a good friend and I spent a good deal of time at In-N-Out Burger arguing over whether the single hamburger is better than the double-double. Trivial, yes. Useful for instruction or edification? Absolutely not. Tons of fun? Unquestionably. Some points of opposition will be insignificant, but others may be substantial. And each time we encounter them is an opportunity for the friendship to be deepened, for each person's commitment to seeking understanding to be reinforced, and for love of the truth to take root just a little more deeply in our hearts.

Allow me to repeat one caution, though: we will be tempted to attach ourselves more to our disagreements and our desire to appear "reasonable" in the face of them than to the truthful answers that obligate us to move beyond understanding toward persuasion. My hope is that on fundamental questions, disagreements ultimately go away—because either one or both of us has learned that we were wrong and has changed our stance because of it. But when such intellectual conversions finally happen, the goods that allowed us to disagree well and the friendships they engendered will endure to the end.

9

How to Ask a
Good Question

"Well, now, *that's* a silly question."

And with that, my new homeless friend was off with a breathless destruction of my cheerfully naïve, "How are you?" I hadn't expected a philosophical discourse in return, but that was precisely what Alan gave me.

"That is a question that cannot be answered. What is man, how is man, where is man going? You fancy yourself a philosopher?" (He did not wait for an answer to this.) "Well, these are questions that philosophers have been asking for millennia and no one has found an answer. So the next time you come over here, do your homework and ask about the history of Epiphany or what we should do with the monarchy."

---

1. Karl Barth, *The Christian Life: Church Dogmatics IV, 4 Lecture Fragments* (London; New York: T. & T. Clark, 2004), 246.

Not only had Alan established himself as one of the most intelligent homeless people I've ever had the pleasure of talking to, but he had reminded me of a key lesson: there are in fact silly questions. "No stupid questions" is the cliché that sanctifies every effort, that emboldens even the most timid to put their questions to the world. And inasmuch as it signals a welcome to questioning, that's okay. But as Alan clearly reminded me, even those who write books on the practice of questioning still have something to learn.

The wise risk looking foolish and ask their questions, while the proud stay silent. More often than not, we're held back from asking our questions because we think they are "obvious" and that we're the only ones in the room who have them. But such "obvious questions" are often the most difficult to answer. Why does something fall to the ground? It took a long time for someone to figure out the math behind gravity. What are we made of? Where do our dreams come from? What is justice? Socrates wasn't the wisest man in Athens for demonstrating his vast knowledge but for having the courage to pose his questions even at great personal cost. Those who love understanding risk their reputations to pursue it. Only the haughty and the dead never have a question reach their lips.

There are questions that do not *fit*, though. As a teacher, I didn't care whether the students' first questions were any good: I simply wanted them to be interested enough to ask them. My coaching and prodding about quality came later, in the middle of their practice, as they learned to recognize when they'd asked a doozy and when they . . . hadn't. As they became more familiar with the method, we would sometimes reflect about what made some questions fit better than others.

Being able to tell the difference between a fitting and infelicitous question is a little like telling the difference between good and bad music. We don't simply value Mendelsohn's Branden-burg Concerti because they happen to be old. We recognize that they are excellent representatives of their form. Were I to record my meager efforts on the piano, we wouldn't ignore them simply because I was the one banging them out: they would rightly fall to the dustbin of history because, however noble my intentions, they'd still be no good.

There is a similar sort of practiced art to questioning, a pru-dential knowledge about when to ask a question, what question to ask, how to ask it, and so on. Lawyers and investigators learn how to become excellent questioners because they need to elicit unique sets of information. Every doctor starts his diagnosis with an inquiry and how they go about it significantly affects our ex-perience. Reporters go to school to question well because their livelihood depends upon it. Teachers sometimes take classes in how to question well and are (thankfully!) starting to take classes in how to help their students question well.[2] The practice is more art than science, but we still have plenty to learn.

As we grow in our discernment of questions, we start to hear the shades and subtleties at work in the form. When someone asks a question that goes to the heart of the matter and asks it sin-cerely, it *feels* different. It will cut through a conversation with the clarity of a bell. Think about being in the boardroom when some-one voices the question that everyone felt but no one had quite articulated: the transformation in those moments is almost physi-cally palpable. Everyone leans in and focuses a little more.[3] The

2. Dan Rothstein and Luz Santana, *Make Just One Change: Teach Students to Ask Their Own Questions* (Cambridge, MA: Harvard Education Press, 2011).

3. As in, literally leans in. You can tell when people are really engaged in their ques-tions because their body betrays them. Just like any public speaker can tell when an audience really cares what he has to say—their posture and physical presence gives them away.

phenomenon is almost like hounds who have caught the scent. We wait and search, and wait and search, but when the trail is found—away we go.

How Questions Arise

Questions arise when our sense of the *whole* collides with a *part* that is new. I first realized this as a student in the Torrey Honors Institute, where we would spend three-hour chunks dialoguing together about great books. Since some classes were more productive than others, I wanted to know *why*. So I diagnosed each session that we had, evaluating the conversation and my role in it. In all the best sessions, we would bounce back and forth between the meaning of the whole text and close readings of specific passages, reinterpreting our understanding of each in light of the others. In that process, we came to a better understanding of the text and the realities the text pointed to—even if the text failed to truthfully depict them.

Whole, part, whole. Our sense of the whole is, of course, limited and imperfect. And the people and ideas, events and encounters that we experience often surprise us and don't fit our categories. We learn when we see new things or see old things in a new light. But it is that attempt to make sense of the phenomenon before us in light of our preexisting understanding that generates inquiries. Either our limited grasp of the whole can already explain the phenomenon or not—but through the encounter we sharpen our understanding both of the whole and the part.

Let me put a finer point on it: I spent eighteen months working as a financial planner before I discerned my vocation elsewhere. During that time, I would sit with my clients and talk with them about their plans for the future while evaluating their financial histories and their current resources. My job was to try to find a

path forward for them—to make sense of their story and to provide advice on which "parts" to fix to get them to the ending they
wanted. But their finances were only a window into the whole
of their lives. Fears, anxieties, cares, and hopes drove so many of
their financial decisions—and the rest of their lives limited what
sort of changes would have been possible. To properly and re-
sponsibly provide reasonable recommendations about the part, I
had to attempt to see their finances in light of their whole story.
Sometimes when clients would start talking, significant wounds
came up and financial advising teetered on the edge of becoming
life counseling.

The same whole-part-whole idea worked out in a different
direction during that season as well. Those were the eighteen
months between January of 2008 and June of 2009, which was the
worst financial crisis that many of my clients had ever seen. Like
everyone else, my clients were shell-shocked; they didn't know
how to make sense of losing half of their wealth in light of their
understanding of the markets. And the platitudes we were told
to repeat to answer their questions—the markets always bounce
back, we are in this for the long term—sounded ludicrously hol-
low.[4] As a rookie in the industry, I knew I had only one hope: to
understand what had transpired and reframe my clients' perspectives in light of it. I talked to and learned more about the financial
markets during that season than I ever would have had the markets behaved well. But it was the same principle: in light of the
new, almost unexplainable events, our awareness of the whole
needed to change.

Good questions emerge slowly. It takes time for the whole to
unfold for us. We don't have much of an outline when we set

---

4. I left the industry in part because I found myself unable to say these things, uncertain as I was (and am!) that they are true.

out, and even as we go it's always partial and imperfect. And the meaning is not static, either, as it might be in a novel or a play. We may choose to sacrifice our time for the children's center down the road one day. But if on the next we choose to tell everyone about our good deed, we corrode the quality of our serving as much as we inflate our own ego. The moment of bragging calls into question the integrity of our reasons for serving to begin with. Many of the most significant moments in our lives will not be clear to us until long after they have passed, but their final meaning will not be fixed until death. Only then will we know for sure whether the play will end in redemption or tragedy. And each of our decisions and all that they bring about will be read through that lens. Only when we pass through that veil will the whole of our lives be made complete.

And yet the paradox of the Christian life is that we are *given* a whole life to interpret our lives through, and so the uncertainty that our own death reminds us of can be driven out by the confidence we have in His. Christ has died, Christ is risen, Christ will come again—interpreting our fragmentary moments requires integrating them into *that* narrative, to see how the meaning of Christ's life shapes and determines the meaning of each moment of our own. We can live with the partiality of our lives because we have the fullness of God's. We can live the questions, we might say, because we have an answer who is life Himself. As we explore our experience in light of the Scriptures, we are driven back to the Scriptures with a new thirst for understanding. And through that process of exile and return, of experience and interpretation, our questioning and understanding of God and His world will take us to depths of love and joy and pain and sorrow that we never thought possible.

FOR EVERY QUESTION A MOMENT

Learning to question well demands seeing how our questions fit the context before us. Contrary to the objection of my friend Alan, "How are you?" is a perfectly fine inquiry upon meeting someone: it's pleasant and open-ended, so as to not be threatening. Yes, it may be too cursory, a token offering that doesn't convey sincere interest. But when sincerely asked, the question signals an open invitation for conversation. The question affords the other person maximum flexibility to answer as they please.[5]

What's more, asking "How are you?" of a friend who is suffering is fitting as well. The inflection will be a little different—a little more care, a little more deliberation. Accent on the "are." The stress indicates a serious concern for the other's well-being, but leaves it open for him to respond as he wants—including taking the conversation away from his pain, too. A more specific, pointed question may be appropriate later but not straightaway.

Yet sometimes people have a tin ear for questions. They make inquiries that simply don't fit the context or timing. One of the most hilariously egregious examples I can remember was at a mixer upon just arriving at Oxford as an undergraduate. A good friend and I were introducing ourselves to a particularly energetic girl, who turned to my friend and said, "And what are your deepest hopes and dreams?" I turned away and tried to contain my laughter while my friend graciously responded, "That is *way* too invasive a question for someone that you've just met. That's like a 10 on the intimacy scale, and we're at about a 1.5." It was beautiful. And awkward. And hilarious.

Disciplined hearts and minds will hew close to the questions embedded in the texts and contexts before them. My wife likes

---

5. Compare with the time I met someone who introduced himself as director of AT&T's coverage in the St. Louis area. "Oh," I replied, "so are you the one responsible for all my dropped calls?" Not the most delicate moment of my life.

to occasionally remind me of one of our first sessions together as freshmen. In the middle of a conversation about *The Iliad*, I protested, somewhat loudly and dramatically, "But what *is* Beauty?"[6] I, having no recollection of this event, unfortunately have no reason to doubt my wife's.[7] My only consolation is that I'm sure it wasn't the worst question I asked during our classes together, only she's forgotten all the others.

"What is beauty?" is a good question to ask. It's one of the fundamental questions, a "hard question" that deserves our attention. Yet I opened the line of inquiry at the wrong time and in the wrong way. Approaching "hard questions" too quickly can be a sign of pseudo-intellectual pretentiousness, not intellectual maturity. For young minds like mine, it's enough to set about considering Homer's conception of friendship in Patroclus and Achilles because it's closer to the text. "What is beauty?" may be buried somewhere down there but, if it is, I wasn't going to get there without a lot of jimmy rigging and artificial reading. Asking obvious, surface questions when we are starting out allows us to establish a broader base of knowledge to explore in deeper, more interesting ways later on. We start from where we are, after all, and usually that's on the surface.

Reducing every conversation to a few Big Questions like I did is pretty normal for those getting their intellectual sea legs under them. It's no slight to Calvinists and Arminians to point out that there are other questions theology pursues besides those that arise from the collision of free will and God's sovereignty.[8] Yet eager, energetic young students of the discipline tend to reduce every line of inquiry to that one. Otherwise interesting discussions

---

6. Loudly and dramatically is how I roll.

7. I mentioned to my wife that I was including this story. Her response: "Wow, you're really going to confess everything in this book, eh?" We take questioning *seriously* in our household.

8. Like my personal favorite, that of the doctrine of *communicatio idiomatum*!

on the incarnation will careen into intractable arguments over the meaning of double predestination. There is a time and place for thinking through that relationship: but that time and place is often later and somewhere else.[9]

Which is to say, questioning well means having the discipline to pursue a line of inquiry without yielding to the impulse to wander every which way on a whim. The steadiness of intellectual determination can help us push through the difficulties and unclarities before us without necessarily returning to terrain that feels more comfortable and familiar. The path exploring God's goodness may eventually lead through disputes about Paul's meaning of "predestined," but that doesn't mean we necessarily have to take them up right away.[10] There are a host of other texts and ways of approaching the question other than through that (very important!) lens. The threads that we *do not* pick up and follow are just as significant as those that we do.

Questioning well also means the question fits the things questioned as much as the moment. Over the past few years, I've taken to opening conversations with some of my younger married friends with a knowing, "Well, you're still married?" It's a gently worded, slightly facetious inquiry that is meant to bring a smile while opening up a conversation about the challenges and joys they are discovering in marriage. I've had people respond with everything from, "Yes, and loving it!" to a nervous "Yes, barely." The question fits the person: I only ask it to friends, and friends that I know *are* still married. If I knew they weren't anymore, I'd never ask it. It's a starter question and so deliberately broad. And

---

9. Just so we're clear, I love Calvinists and Arminians. And my own bad habit has been to take every line of inquiry and head straight for the doctrine of creation, as I'm just convinced it's gonna solve a lot of problems.

10. It is not a bad practice to bracket some passages that are more familiar to us to spend more time with those that are not.

my point is to set a low bar for them to jump over, to let them know that I care about their marriage and that they can tell me how things are.

QUESTIONING THE PRACTICAL
AND THE PRACTICE OF QUESTIONING

This is the point where I am supposed to get very practical about how to ask good questions and how not to. How then shall we live? If ever there was a question to which Christians these days want a specific answer, it is that one. Programs and projects are in, while ambiguities and thinking through the practical implications of teaching for ourselves is not.

I should note that I have a good deal of reluctance about providing practical guidance. I worry that our current emphasis on "practical application" is actually contributing to our immaturity. The Word cannot be reduced to principles. It creates a way of seeing the world that we enter into and look through. Scripture is not "applied" to our lives. We live within its domains. The more we saturate ourselves in Scripture's language, the more we will find ourselves inquiring well. In the same way that our dependency on study guides has undermined our ability to be robust communities of questioning, our reliance on application has short-circuited our discernment and deliberation.

It's true that not having more specific "how-tos" can be frustrating. (Think of my poor students and their pleading for "answers!") When I wrote *Earthen Vessels*, many people wanted me to come out and answer precisely whether I thought tattoos are permissible. Right or wrong: that is the question we apparently care most about. But I wanted to think long and hard about a different question, namely, why are tattoos popular? How did marking our bodies with ink become an option that we seriously consider? Why are tattoos mainstream in American culture, and what does their acceptance say about the church's relationship to the world? What does a tattoo mean, anyway, if it means anything at all? I attempted to discern the fundamental presuppositions beneath the phenomenon and in so doing wanted readers to think along with me and then make up their own minds. What does it say about us that we are so eager to have the practical questions answered rather than exploring the world they emerge out of?[11]

But I will make a few recommendations explicit that are, I think, already buried in the previous pages. Like all practices, learning to question well can only properly be done from within. "The beginning of wisdom is: Acquire wisdom."[12] We might say the same about questioning well. If we will set out exploring while remaining attentive to our questions, we will start to see how our inquiries shape our conversations. A broad question—"How are you?"—leaves the whole conversational field open before us while a narrow one sets a very small frame to work within.

As a matter of wisdom, questioning well is an *intentional* practice. It is one way in which the love God has placed in our hearts takes shape within our lives and communities. Questioning well takes a good deal of prudence; it involves knowing the right question to ask at the right time and knowing when not to ask a question at all. And it demands inquiring in such a way that the inquiry leads ourselves and others into a deeper understanding of truth and into gratitude for the gracious kindness of God. The point is not simply to master a craft or a discipline—to perfect a *technique*—but through our questioning to become the sort of people who reflect the love,

---

11. This is a false dichotomy, of course, but the priority matters. The fact that so many people start with the question of whether they are right or wrong suggests a habit of mind primarily ordered toward knowing what to do rather than exploring the presuppositions of our world and our actions in it.

12. Proverbs 4:7 (NASB).

joy, peace, patience, kindness, goodness, faithfulness, gentleness, and self-control that comes from living within the Spirit.[13] Do our inquiries reflect those fruits? Do they engender those fruits in us and others?

Those are not idle questions. As we examine our own questioning as part of our learning to question well, we will find that our inquiries are shaped by our virtues and vices—and inculcate such virtues and vices in us as well. It does not matter whether our inquiries come in the quiet uncertainty of our hearts or the dialogues with our pastors or the small group discussions at our church or in the boardroom at our work. The questions we send into the world reveal and reinforce ourselves and our interests. We may be too self-absorbed to risk looking bad by asking the questions we're interested in. Or we may be too self-absorbed to ask anything else. But if practiced without repentance, both errors further inscribe our self-absorption in us.

Paradoxically, then, we should embrace the failure of the cross in our inquiry and "inquiry badly," which is a spin on Martin Luther's famous dictum "sin boldly." By being willing to fail—to experiment and pose questions that are met with blank stares or that go nowhere—we are freed to learn to question well without the pressure of perfection. Only such a freedom is not for recklessness or foolishness but for the unyielding pursuit of truth. Those who have the courage necessary to question well will desire the truth like water and drink their errors like wine, learning from them and sharpening their understanding after them.[14] It is precisely that sort of courage that the cross releases, for there we

---

13. For that reason, I am avoiding putting down a list of questions and their types here. In a world dominated by techniques, such a list stands in danger of becoming a checklist. For just such a list, I commend my friend and professor Fred Sanders's list here: http://www.patheos.com/blogs/scriptorium/2011/10/whats-a-good-question/.

14. Using Chesterton's famous formula, of course, that those who have courage "desire life like water and yet drink death like wine."

remember that the God who saved us will also sanctify us, in His timing and His way. All will be well, one way or the other.

Questioning is a communal practice and cannot be done without the help and sharpening of friends. Finding fellow explorers of the world (and becoming better friends through our mutual exploration) will help us confront our sense of entitlement to answers and our proclivities toward defensiveness that often stand beneath our inquiries. We cannot easily isolate our questions from the rest of our lives, after all. Questioning is a practice through which our entire lives take form. Questioning with those who know us well and who can gently challenge us will help ensure that our questions remain rooted in faith seeking understanding.

Fortunately, we travel into the unknown with the company of the saints and the practices of worship that guide and structure the church's fellowship. Our local church communities, instead of on blogs or at conferences, should be where the hardest questions about the Bible are pursued (rather than passed over). Pastors who skip the controversial or difficult questions beneath the texts in favor of practical applications aren't simply doing an injustice to the text; they are implicitly communicating that such questions are "off-limits" and so undermining the confidence people have that Scripture will stand up to close scrutiny. We can only question well within our communities if we question courageously, which means exploring issues on which there is the possibility for confusion, disagreement, and error.

Yet silence is the aspect of our inquiry that may matter more than all the others. Silence is a form of negative space in the conversation: we are only as comfortable with the unknown as we are able to sit quietly. The small group at church should be the place where we learn to be comfortable with not knowing what to say about Scripture rather than grabbing at the nearest clichés to get through it. We cannot inquire well if we have not the patience to sit through the discomfort of being quiet. I would often allow conversations during my classes to fade into moments of silence for as long as was necessary before someone had something interesting to say. As a good rule of thumb, not filling every pause with a question or statement is one of the first practices and habits that good discussion leaders need to inculcate—and the rest of us as well.

Similarly, we should be willing to face the prospect of being bored in a conversation. We want the perpetual stimulation of our minds, but that's partly because we've been badly formed. Conversations are a microcosm of life. And if we are not able to discipline our minds to stay on one subject for an hour without hopping around, then our conversations and inquiries will stay in the shallows. Boredom is the beginning of our learning, not the end, for it is the moment when we run out of thoughts in our own head and have to attend again to the text or world before us and inquire in new ways. I once spent sixteen weeks reading Philippians twice a day. It was the most exhausting, tiring, and mind-numbing reading I have ever done—but it also fundamentally reformed my life. I became so familiar with the book that everything in my life was somehow connected to it. Had I not pushed through my boredom and reread the text more times than I could stomach, I would have never encountered its power in the way that I did.

The practice of repetitive reading and dialoguing is best done, though, within a community. I have long wanted to see church small groups read a passage of Scripture slowly and repetitively, sometimes out loud and sometimes silently, until they have exhausted all the questions that can be asked about it—and the text has exhausted them with all the questions *it* poses to us. Such a practice would involve (of course!) jettisoning the ready-baked study guides. But it would also embed the Word far more deeply in the minds and hearts of the hearers and break through the surface answers and clichés that we often allow to stop thought.

The practice itself would inculcate as much virtue as it would demand of us. Reading slowly, deliberately, and patiently is crucial to questioning well—whether we are "reading" our lives, or books, or the people around us. We should allow our minds the freedom to linger, to immerse themselves in what we are considering, and to explore its nooks and crannies. Love is patient, after all, and not only when the object of our affections doesn't behave as we want.

Similarly, we should broaden the horizons of questions we can ask by reading and thinking more diversely than we do. One reason to read historical books is that their ways of framing the world were not our ways, nor were their questions our questions. As we encounter those differences and discover surprising similarities, our own understanding of the whole is put into tension with questions that wouldn't naturally emerge from it. People who read only literature written by the living will have a much more difficult time experiencing that dissonance, as most of our writing is aimed at addressing the questions of our own day. But by inhabiting a new way of seeing the world, we momentarily displace our questions with new ones, which helps us see negative spaces in our own understanding that we may have missed otherwise.

And by reading works from previous generations, we are more easily able to take on virtues that our own does not cultivate. Take my own work as a writer. I know well why writers and pastors read C. S. Lewis. I have read him for years and am an ardent admirer. But my love for Lewis moved me to read what he read, to learn from those who taught him. The only way we become like those we love is through imitation, which means not resting content with the answers they provide but learning to ask the questions that they asked. To make the point theologically, the only way we can think like Jesus thought is by reading what Jesus read and asking the questions He would have asked from it—which is why the Marcionist rejection or suspicion of the Old Testament is a damnable, soul-destroying heresy.

THE PERSISTENCE OF QUESTIONING

Questioning well demands patience and persistence. It is not always obvious what we are missing, though as we grow older and learn more, we slowly realize how little we actually understand. The process of deliberating and inquiring, of searching out and seeking, does not flourish amid hastiness and urgency.

We must be prepared to travel slowly and to not be discouraged if we do not feel we go at all. Sometimes the darkness comes upon us, which is, as T. S. Eliot puts it, "the darkness of God." When our understanding seems to collapse and we feel the weight of our unknowing, when our encounters undo our answers and we know not in which direction to turn—that is the moment when we remember we are kept by the hand of God and to wait until we are drawn "into another intensity, for a further union, a deeper communion."[15] We will all one day enter the darkness of death, the negative space between now and resurrection. Yet the faith, hope, and love we have in the one who has already searched out the "undiscovered country" will keep us safe within His hands until the end of all things, an end that is our beginning.

---

15. Eliot, Four Quartets.

10

The End of
Our Exploring

———— ⟨ ⟩ ————

What have I started? What have I done?
—TREE OF LIFE [1]

"But their eyes were kept from recognizing him." It's so easy to overlook, that passive voice. It's tucked away in plain sight, hidden on the surface. *By whom* were their eyes kept from recognizing Him? And why on earth, or in heaven, would the two disciples traveling down the road to Emmaus be inhibited from seeing their risen Lord?

Luke 24:13–35 is something of an enigma, which makes it a staple in books of this sort. It comes in a questionable shape. It's the sort of passage that evokes wonder and just a little confusion. The resurrected Jesus appears to two disciples who are locked in conversation about the events surrounding His passion as they travel the seven-mile journey from Jerusalem to Emmaus. Jesus

---

1. Terrence Malick, *Tree of Life*, directed by Terrence Malick (Los Angeles: River Road Entertainment, 2011).

enters into their conversation, allowing them to recount to Him the events of His life. But His response is chastisement: "Oh foolish ones, and slow of heart to believe all that the prophets have spoken. Was it not necessary that the Christ should suffer these things and enter into his glory?"[2] Jesus answers His own question by conducting a comprehensive Old Testament study, showing them "in all the Scriptures the things concerning himself."

But why veil their eyes so that they cannot recognize Him? The curiosities don't stop there; after He ends the lesson, Jesus acts like He's going to leave. The possibility of His absence (even though they do not yet recognize Him) moves the disciples to plead with Him to stay longer. They eat together, and in that communion meal their eyes are finally opened to see their Savior. Only through the breaking of bread, the joint sharing of life do they find the final satisfaction of their desire to understand the meaning of the Passion events.

For these disciples, a truthful interpretation of the Scriptures isn't sufficient. Having the right answer is necessary, but not enough. Even in the witness of the Scriptures, Jesus points forward to the final disclosure, the *consummation* of knowledge. The understanding we gain here and now is not false, even if it has not yet been brought to completion. The biblical instruction both intensifies their desire and prepares them for the revelation. Jesus gives them an outline so they will recognize Him when they see in full. Faithful interpretation prepares us for a communion that goes beyond it, a peace that transcends all understanding.

Here we see, also, that Jesus is willing to hide Himself that He may be known. He renders Himself not-known that their desire for Him would increase. He hides Himself in their conversation so He might reveal Himself in communion. The light shines in

---

2. Luke 24:26 (ESV).

the darkness, but it is a light that overpowers mortal eyes and makes them blind. The immortal, invisible, only wise God "dwells in unapproachable light."[3] As the old hymn put it, it's only "the splendour of light [that] hideth thee."[4] For what seem to us now negative spaces will one day be uncovered and our eyes strengthened so that we are able to see that the glory of God permeates even the darkest parts of our world.

What the passage says raises enough questions on its own. But more provocative is what it does not say. As Jesus hides Himself from the disciples, so Luke hides Jesus' interpretation of the Old Testament from us. The one definitive, infallible, finally authoritative reading of the Old Testament, from the mouth of Jesus Himself—and Luke does not bother to write it down. It is almost as though he is unwilling to short-circuit the process of learning for us. He leaves Jesus' teaching in the shadows so that we ourselves may be moved to inquire and explore until the last day, when all shall permanently come into the light.

THE END OF OUR EXPLORING

I have sat in empty streets and watched by lamplight while others retreat to their beds. I have felt the pangs of sorrow, the tragic joys of an inexpressible beauty. I have sat listening, quietly, to the thoughtless chatter of the television and wondered whether I am any different. I have felt the oddness of a church pew, have tripped and stumbled while walking forward to break bread in gratitude. I have wondered about that little church down the street and whether it will be boarded up someday. And whether I will survive it. I have felt the groaning of a question that I have not yet found the words for. I have longed for the newness, the

---

3. 1 Timothy 6:16 (ESV).
4. "Immortal, Invisible, God Only Wise," written by Walter C. Smith in 1876.

remaking, and have wondered why He tarries. I have trembled at the gravity of writing down words. Will I too join Him on the last day? What must I do to be saved? I know the cold of a night beneath the terror of eternity.

When we stand before the face of God, shall we dare ask a question? How shall our voices find words, much less inquiring ones? When we see the suffering of the infants, the brutality of a violent world, how can we have a thought at all? Shall we tarry here, and linger over one last cup of tea? Is it vanity to believe our words have found a meaning, or that a meaning has found our words? Shall we speak, or shall we sit in the silence, measuring out our lives by the subtle smiles we pass each other across our open books? Is it because of all that quietness that libraries are such romantic places, or is it that we feel ourselves daunted by the surrounding mysteries?

It is a long journey, this road home. There are detours and wrong turns, mistakes and sins. There is repenting, always repenting, and a mercy that stands with, in, and around us. And there is growth, the only law of the life of the Spirit. It is not always perceptible, for the seeds beneath the earth are reborn long before we see their shoots. And it is always painful, for except that a seed fall to the ground and die, it can bear no fruit. But still there is expansion, the stretching outward and upward to the heavens. We grow into sight. But we are not given it yet. We have heard the echo, but we have not grasped its source. We have seen the reflection, but we await the consummation.

When shall I come and appear before my God?

Questioning is one form our longing takes. We search out the earth for satisfaction, roaming like Odysseus until we too reach our home. We talk together, wondering on the path toward Emmaus. It is a journey of a thousand sorrows and of a thousand joys.

And sometimes the joys and the sorrows come together, and are found within each other, in a collision like a cross that sends our wonder soaring to new heights.

We question beneath a shadow that our eyes are too weak to penetrate. It is like the shadow of death but has become in the resurrection the shadow of incomprehensible life. It is not because He is a conjuror playing the hoax that Jesus vanishes from His disciples. They are not ready for the permanence, not large enough to see the expansiveness of His beauty. They must undergo the purification of their desires before the revelation occurs. Yet when it comes: "No eye has seen," Paul says, "nor ear has heard." Or dare I say Shakespeare's translation is better? For it comes in the stammering of someone who has had a foretaste: "The eye of man hath not heard, the ear of man hath not seen, man's hand is not able to taste, his tongue to conceive, nor his heart to report what my dream was."[5]

I sometimes wonder whether I use the questions to forestall the answers, to procrastinate and delay. The satisfaction of our desires comes with the trumpet blast of judgment. At the unveiling is a pronouncement, the final division between *this* and *that*. The answer closes things off, giving us only the choice to live within reality or construct one of our own. To be answered, to have our questions resolved, makes us accountable for all that we have sought out. An answer provides closure, an ending, allows the curtains to fall.

Yet the vision we are given is a person who goes beyond the answer even while including it in Himself. It is not a framework, an understanding that will make us whole but a *Who*. The authorized witness points to the man Jesus, the man back to the words

5. William Shakespeare, *A Midsummer Night's Dream* (New York: Washington Square Press, 1993), 136.

that He makes life. Like those disciples, we stand in danger of resting at the one while missing the other. But the final question we will be asked is not what account we are able to provide but what person we are able to plead to.

Until then: "We shall not cease from exploration."[6] Old men really *must* be explorers, for if they are not, who among us can be saved? We young in our pursuits are ever in danger of merely being childish. We are not yet strong enough to be childlike. That is for the wise, for those who have gone before us, who have come to their end and found themselves for the first time there, the end that is always a new beginning and a renewing of our exploration. As T. S. Eliot goes on, in the passage from which the title of this book is taken:

> And the end of all our exploring
> Will be to arrive where we started
> And know the place for the first time.
> Through the unknown, remembered gate
> When the last of earth left to discover
> Is that which was the beginning;
> At the source of the longest river
> The voice of the hidden waterfall
> And the children in the apple-tree
> Not known, because not looked for
> But heard, half heard, in the stillness
> Between the two waves of the sea.
> Quick now, here, now, always—
> A condition of complete simplicity
> (Costing not less than everything)

---

6. Excerpt from "Little Gidding" from *Four Quartets* by T. S. Eliot. Copyright 1942 by Houghton Mifflin Harcourt Publishing Company; copyright© renewed 1970 by T. S. Eliot. Reprinted by permission of Houghton Mifflin Harcourt Publishing Company. All rights reserved.

And all shall be well and
All manner of things shall be well
When the tongues of flame are in-folded
Into the crowned knot of fire
 And the fire and the rose are one.[7]

To arrive where we started. To return to our home, only to find it new, deeper, and more perfect. To see anew goods that we had buried and forgotten in the dimness of our vision. The setting sun on the limestone, the fog fading into the frost on a winter day, the tender smiles between the elderly couple across the table—to be awake to see the world's resplendent goodness, a beauty that will somehow overwhelm all the horrors of the night. To encounter the face of another, containing within it the mysteries of a soul in which is the image of God. To see in the breaking of the bread the vision of the risen Lord. "And we beheld his glory, the glory as of the only begotten of the Father."[8] God comes as a stranger into His own home, that we might again have a home with Him.

The end of our exploring and our path through the far-off country are one and the same. "For to me, to live is Christ."[9] But to die, that too is Christ. And to inquire and to fail, these also must be Christ. We ask our questions beneath that sentence, a sentence that seems like death but is really abundance. The reason for our desire is its consummation, the joy that goes ever onward, always forward. The defining passage of St. Paul's life and ministry is not found in the argument of Romans or the majestic panoramas of Ephesians but in the heartfelt intimacy of his letter to the Philippians: "I press on toward the goal for the prize of the

---

7. Ibid., 208–9.
8. John 1:14 (KJV).
9. Philippians 1:21 (ESV).

upward call of God in Christ Jesus." [10] The prize is not stasis but a movement toward the infinite center, the depths of the goodness of God in the face of Jesus Christ. Only then is our movement outward, into and toward the world that radiates with His glory, to take our place among the chorus of creatures endlessly singing the praises of His glory. But in all and through all, the infinite explosion of abundant goodness because of our union with Christ.

For the answer we are given is the life of a person, the Lord of all, life abundantly. Shall I say this again? As we sit across the table, wondering, "How can these things be?" we are interrupted by the intimate laughter of a joke worn thin by retelling, by the chair that breaks on the unsuspecting guest, by the breaking of bread and the candles and a conversation that's lasted well beyond midnight. "But now I call you friends," He tells us. And so we shall be friends indeed.

But for now, there is the plodding, the questioning and the prayer, the serving and the sacrifice, the living within friendship while we look for the King's return. Certainty is a charlatan, doubt a deceiver. The steadfast confidence of faith kneels between, neither triumphant nor defeated but possessed by a sober goodness, a joyful sorrow too powerful for the words that might bear it: "Thy kingdom come, thy will be done." Assurance and conviction, that we are kept not by ourselves or our ideas but by the One who is Lord of all. The invisible made visible within the land of the living. And in the space between the advents, before the end of our exploring comes upon us, we freely explore the "all things" we are given in Christ and learn, ploddingly and patiently, to see them as He does. "For thine is the kingdom." Foreigners in a strange land, longing to be taken home—yes. But also strangers encountering our own home, seeing it under the ruin of sin and praying for its

10. Philippians 3:14 (ESV).

renewal. But here and now, always, a confidence in the God who acts, the God who saves, the God who comes to us in the person of Jesus Christ: "For thine is the power."

All this is the life of faith. It is hope that marks our witness, the confidence that beneath the felt absence of God from our lives and world, the promise of His presence is gloriously, permanently, belligerently, and unyieldingly true. His promise is a *fact*—in the beginning was the Word, the Word beneath and before all things, the fact who is the wellspring of understanding and the source of all joy. And within the promise, our exploring is moved by prayer and our strength renewed and consummated in worship. "For thine is the glory." And Abraham grew strong in faith, with a strength that is offered to us all. Here is the end of our exploring: the God who rose again will one day return and make all things new. We look for the glorious finality of His appearing, when we shall be finally like Him for we shall see Him as He is. And in the meantime, we wait for the tongues of purification and of prayer, of fire and of friendship to descend upon us—for all the facts of joy to take root in our lives and bring forth the fruit that will endure to eternal life. For from Him and through Him and to Him be all things, all glory and honor, all praise and worship, all searching and finding, "world without end." Faith and hope and love—abide these three, abide in increase and growth and expansion, now and forever. For to those who are given, *more will be added.* "Amen."

The following appendices were originally
published as essays at Boundless.org, a web journal for
young adults by Focus on the Family. I am grateful
for their original prompting to write them and for
their permission to republish them here.

How Not to Lose Your Faith in a
Christian College

————— ◦ —————

The greatest threat to my relationship with Jesus in college was . . . college.

You're probably familiar with the horror stories associated with secular universities: the debauchery of dorm life, the loneliness of being the only Christian, the challenge of hostile and derogatory professors, the constant pressure to conform. Secular universities are undoubtedly challenging places for Christians. There's a reason why ministries that prepare high school graduates to thrive at such places have exploded during the last twenty years.

But I didn't go to one of those universities. My time at college wasn't spent warding off the temptations of alcohol or combating secular ideologies in the classroom.

I went to a private Christian university. I was faced with the impossible struggle of deciding whether to attend chapel on Mondays, Wednesdays, and Fridays, or Tuesdays, Thursdays, and Sunday night. We prayed before class, prayed after class, prayed before meals—the really spiritual among us even prayed before bed.

We consumed so much of the Bible in our classes that the university practically handed us a minor in it. And our environment was so unique that we would jokingly refer to the "bubble" that surrounded our beautiful little campus, keeping out the forces of evil and Britney Spears.

OK, so we weren't joking about the bubble; we were convinced it was really there, *Truman Show* style. Some even claimed to see it if they squinted hard enough.

I have fond memories of my time in college. It was incredibly beneficial in ways that I am only now starting to realize. But having the benefit of hindsight, it's also clear to me that I waltzed through my college experience oblivious to some of the hidden challenges and threats it posed to my faith.

A FIRM FOUNDATION

When I left for college, I had one mission: build a "firm foundation." I looked at those four years as a period of intense theological and pastoral training, and I was *determined* to set myself up for a lifetime of spiritual success. I was going to leave behind the moral failures of high school and finally reach maturity as a Christian.

That language—of building a firm foundation for our faith—is pretty common for students heading into Christian universities. And there is something admirable about it. It conveys a sense of longing for stability and depth in our relationships with God. And those are precisely the sorts of qualities we should pursue.

But it also obscures a deep fact about the nature of Christian faith, a fact that undermines the language of foundations: We don't get to build the foundation of our faith. If anything, it's built for us. To switch the metaphors, faith is a *gift*, not something we buy for ourselves.

In Scripture, when gifts are given we're expected to do something with them. When Luke tells the parable of the talents, the steward gives the servants money, then chastises one of them for not increasing what he was given. The same applies to faith: When given, it engenders a desire and an obligation to *cultivate* it. Paul can speak in one sentence of the fact that his justification comes from outside of himself, and switch to earnest and passionate language about *pursuing* the prize of the upward call of God in the next.

But the one thing we're incapable of doing is *building* the foundation. At best, we participate in building the house on top. (But even so, "Unless the Lord builds the house, they labor in vain who build it"; Psalm 127:1.)

What does this have to do with keeping your faith in a Christian college? Plenty. Because the foundation is not of our own making, we should not approach the issue out of a fearful anxiety. Instead, we can be courageous, taking into account not only our weakness as Christians and the reality of a spiteful adversary, but the triumph of the resurrection of Jesus and His empowering Holy Spirit.

A HOLY INTENTIONALITY

When people go off to secular universities or colleges, they know what they're getting themselves into. Judging by the increase of enrollment at Christian universities, I'd say we have done a pretty good job of warning folks about the challenges and dangers of secular higher education.

But the awareness of those dangers allows for—and requires—a significant degree of intentionality if Christians aim to flourish in a secular environment. Because the institutional pressures are working against cultivating a robust faith, maintaining one requires the discipline of structuring your life to make room for a deep relationship with God.

But in a Christian college, it's easy to let the environment do all the spiritual heavy lifting. Like it did for me. I did my chapel time. I prayed before classes. I even talked to the occasional non-Christian or two on the weekends (conversations that went something like, "Decaf venti white-chocolate mocha. Thanks"). Christianity—and the peculiar language of "Christianese"—*pervaded* the atmosphere. As a result, I struggled to carve out time to cultivate the spiritual disciplines of solitude, silence, Scripture intake, and fasting.

In other words, Christian colleges enable students to confuse the culture with the relationship, which empowers external factors to take precedence. I'm all for Christian community, and the friendships I gained during my time in college are still the deepest I have. But there is no substitute for quiet contemplation of God in His Word and through prayer. And the easy and pervasive spirituality of the Christian college environment can dull our awareness of our sin, and even more foundational, our need for grace.

I eventually wearied of the environment and longed to get beyond "the bubble." Chapel went from welcome refreshment as a freshman to dreary drudgery as a senior. By the end, I was no longer grateful for the opportunity (of a lifetime!) to worship communally multiple times a week and to be fed by the preaching of God's Word. I was required to go, so I went. And if the sermon or the worship didn't meet my standards, well, I had both barrels loaded with biblical information (thanks, Bible classes!) to critique and dismiss the speaker.

But my irritation had nothing to do with the godly frustration of being inside a cocoon for too long. Instead, I nursed a subtle and pernicious cynicism about the people around me. By the time I was a senior, I had no desire to go to chapel and hear one more bad sermon. I couldn't deign to sing another theologically trite worship song. And everywhere I went, I began to distinguish between the *real* Christians (who, like me, managed to be unremittingly depressing in their authenticity) and those who were just *playing the game.*

Cynicism of that sort isn't simply a lie about the world or the people around us. In my case, it was grounded in a false view of my own spiritual maturity that was quickly exposed when I left the Christian college environment. As I entered the "real world," it became clear that I had failed those four years to build the disciplines and habits of the spiritual life in the way that I would have had to do in a secular environment. But rather than appreciating the environment and maximizing it through cultivating personal holiness, I sneered at the simplicity of it all and mocked those who didn't "get it."

PART TWO

Let's return for a moment to *why* I went to college: I wanted to deepen my knowledge of God and how He has worked in history. That's a *very* different reason for attending a university than a lot of people will give—especially non-Christians. Colleges advertise themselves as places where students' assumptions about the world will be challenged and their horizons broadened.

That is precisely what a university should do. Mine did it, even though I wasn't looking for that kind of challenge when I went.

When it comes to the most important questions, Christian

college students are in the peculiar situation of being convinced we have the answers *even before we ask the question*. In fact, many of our parents get a little nervous if we start asking questions too seriously—as though questions themselves will inevitably lead us outside the Christian faith.

This belief in the answers, which is right and good, too often leads to platitudes—answers that lack depth and are generally deployed far too early in the conversation. There's a process of questioning for which Christian education needs to allow room.

Let me be perfectly clear: The "Sunday school answers" are true. They correspond to reality. "Jesus loves me" is just about as good an answer as you can get to all the major questions of human existence. We can trust that those answers are true and make all kinds of arguments for them.

But part of the nature of education is to ask deeper and deeper questions and view the answers we discover in new and surprising ways. A platitude cuts off that process, and when handed to students who are honestly struggling with the intellectual foundations of their faith, it tends to make them feel isolated and frustrated.

I've seen firsthand that there are students at Christian colleges who struggle in this way. And occasionally, they get fed up and leave the faith.

Let me be blunt for a moment. When that happens, the effects of sin are almost always at work—effects that reach into a person's mind and distort the way he encounters reality. A lot of times, we derive our energy from what we're *against*, rather than what we're for. I call it "beleaguered minority syndrome" (BMS). When Christians head off to secular universities, they know they will be different from everyone else. That terrifies some people, but for those who suffer from BMS, being different is invigorating. Sometimes it is a type of rebellion, except it's a rebellion *into* the gospel.

But when those who are contrarians at heart—and I certainly am—end up in Christian environments, we work to avoid being "*that* kind of Christian." And occasionally, contrarians find enough to be opposed to that they leave the faith altogether.

While college *is* a time for questioning, it's *not* a time for doubt—at least not how we generally think about it. Questions asked from a posture of seeking understanding are different from those asked from a posture of skepticism. In this sense, doubt isn't benign. How we ask questions is a matter of the heart. Sometimes I would find myself demanding answers rather than seeking answers from a prior position of faith.

Asking questions, then, is essential to a Christian college experience. After all, Christianity *is* true, which means that we can ask our most challenging, most penetrating, most troubling questions. And if we stare at it long enough, we'll see the answer. As some wise guy once said, all who seek, find.

Cultivating Your Faith in a Christian College

How, then, should students cultivate their faith while attending a Christian college? Here are a few tips I would propose:

Cultivate a holy intentionality. Prayer chapels are generally the most underused areas of any college campus. While I would occasionally find my way there, I regret not spending more time cultivating the life of prayer in college.

The same is true of fasting and Bible study. The freedoms of college life make it the best environment many people will ever have to engage in regular fasting and Bible reading. Christian colleges are amazing training grounds to learn about Scripture. But there are different ways of reading Scripture, and studying the

Bible for class is no substitute for saturating our lives with the Word in order to encounter the living God.

Do not give up meeting together. Christian colleges are not churches. They share some of the same features, but they are also one-generational communities that don't generally take communion regularly. While I did go to church during college, I attended four churches in four years, which made it difficult to cultivate the sort of intergenerational fellowship that Scripture says is essential.

Spend time off campus. I don't mean at the mall, shopping. Spend time with real people in their homes. Spend time serving the hurting and loving the lost. Spend time with your family.

Many Christian colleges do a great job of providing means of getting beyond campus, and I wish I had taken greater advantage of them to cultivate the spiritual discipline of service. But even beyond that, college is an artificial environment, and spending time away from campus would have helped me see more clearly the challenges I was facing that were unique to college life.

Be for the gospel, not against those who don't quite get it. Living "for the gospel" means being gracious and charitable toward everyone—including those with whom you disagree. This is the only way to avoid "beleaguered minority syndrome." And it will help you avoid cynicism.

Ask the hardest questions you can, but ask them in a community of friends who love Jesus. I was blessed in my friendships. My friends encouraged me to ask hard questions and were patient with me as I sought answers. Our friendships, our knowledge, and even our faith grew as we rigorously tested Scripture.

Sing praise. My senior year, when I allowed cynicism to take hold of me, my delight in worship slowly eroded. To this day, I can judge my spiritual health by the level of critique and cynicism in my heart during corporate gatherings.

The God of grace calls us, as people, to extend as much grace to those around us as we have been given. If we refuse to do so, we cloud our vision of our own dependency and imperfection. As Harold Best has put it, "A mature Christian is easily edified." That's a lesson that college seniors need to hear.

* * *

Christian colleges are not "hostile environments." In fact, they provide an exceptional context for young adults to grow in knowledge and love. But because of that, the challenges they present are all the more subtle. By conflating my faith with the environment, I grew numb to deeper attitudes of the heart. This led to a sense of pride and cynicism that were only challenged when I traded the safe confines of the Christian college for the implicitly hostile world of business.

At some point amid the excellent training I was receiving, the knowledge I was gaining, and the Christian activity I was enjoying, I forgot the most basic of biblical commands: "Let no man think more highly of himself than he ought" (Romans 12:3).

Christian colleges need to be places where the gospel is repeated and reinforced. We need to be people who remind each other of the gospel, and who seek out friends who will do the same. Keeping the faith in a Christian college ultimately requires a community that is shaped by, and submissive to, Scripture and the Holy Spirit.

Appendix 2

Loving Those
Who Leave

T alk about practicing what I preach.

Not long after I wrote about keeping the faith in a Christian college, a friend and former student emailed me to let me know that he had relinquished his own belief in Jesus. It was surprising news. While I hadn't talked to him for a few months, he is an intelligent fellow from a good home, and I had never detected any movement in that direction.

So there I was, reading his email, wondering how I should respond.

Naturally, I freaked out.

I didn't throw chairs or wring my hands in agony. But I did experience a lot of sadness and anger, and even a fair amount of fear. As his former Bible teacher, I wondered whether there was something I said or did that launched him on this path.

I imagine this sort of reaction is pretty common for Christians when their friends or family members decide to leave behind the faith. After all, Christianity is a belief system—but it is also a host of uniting practices and activities. When someone rejects those, it feels like betrayal.

Of course, describing this transition as a "decision" isn't quite accurate. I decided to follow Jesus in a very different way than I decided what to wear this morning. The latter was done in haste, without very much consideration about the meaning of my clothing (much to my wife's chagrin). But my verbal confession of faith that Jesus is Lord was the culmination of a series of experiences, realizations, and insights that I ultimately found undeniable.

And from what I can tell, going the other direction tends to work the same way. In my friend's case, he found some questions he couldn't answer and had some painful experiences. Brick by brick the wall was built (or, you could say, torn down). And I didn't see it coming.

My worry is that as Christians, we sometimes add a few more bricks to that wall by responding out of insecurity and anger, instead of love, to those who leave the faith. We are called to bear witness to the reality of Christ's love not only for those who have never come to faith but also to those who leave it. With that in mind, I offer this exploration of how to—and how not to—respond when loved ones reject Christianity.

THE APOLOGETICS DOUBLE-BARREL APPROACH

Of all the problematic responses, this is my personal favorite. Maybe it's because I love thinking hard about whether Christianity is true, but every time someone I know has left the faith, I've opened up both barrels of the apologetics gun.

The desire to present the case for Christianity at that moment is understandable. After all, it's a pretty good case. At the same time, the double-barrel approach reduces people to their minds and misunderstands the messy nature of how belief systems actually change. If disbelief—like belief—is the culmination of a process, then no silver-bullet argument will reverse it.

I've been guilty of skipping the crucial step of asking whether they even *want* to discuss the truth of Christianity. Some people simply don't want to have the conversation, at least not right away, and forcing it on them drives an unnecessary wedge in the relationship.

THE MORALITY POLICE APPROACH

For some people, leaving Christianity behind can result in a loosening of their moral code. They may feel a sense of newfound freedom and express it in ways that Christians find problematic.

Of course, sometimes the problem begins much earlier. Some folks who dislike Christianity's ethical demands will hunt for an intellectual justification to rationalize their rejection of it. In these cases, the root problem isn't really a philosophical one, but rather a moral one (which is especially important for Christians who favor the double-barrel apologetic response to keep in mind).

Whatever the case, we as Christians need to realize that it's not our job to play "morality police" and attempt to hold people to a standard with which they no longer agree. After all, their foundation for their moral decisions may be *very* different from ours. The truth about morality must be accompanied by love and grace, lest it unnecessarily reinforce their hostility toward Christians.

THE AWKWARD
CHRISTIAN APPROACH

When my wife and I go out to eat, we'll often pray before our meal. It's always a little awkward, especially when the server drops by with the food in the middle of it. I'm sometimes tempted to alter what I say and hurry through the prayer to prevent an awkward moment.

But prayer is what Christians do. It's part of the heartbeat of our life in Jesus. My tendency to avoid prayer in public isn't grounded in a desire to avoid making others uncomfortable, or a commitment to pray in secret as Jesus commanded, but rather a lack of courage.

I've observed a similar pattern with friends who leave the faith. It's tempting to paper over our differences, to mute the distinct habits and ways of speaking that are a constant reminder of the divisions between us—and the bonds we *used* to share. Sometimes that desire isn't grounded in a sense of hospitality or love for the other person but in a desire to avoid the reminder that things are not the way they once were.

There is a fine line to walk. "Christianese" won't resonate with them anymore, and it's important to be sensitive to that. And it's pretty clear we should avoid undue controversy or divisions with those we love and practice the sort of radical hospitality toward them that distinguishes us as Christians.

But this hospitality must be marked by a quiet confidence that comes from a refusal to compromise the distinctive aspects of our faith. When Peter asked Jesus about the apostle John, Jesus responded: "If I want him to remain until I come, what is that to you? You follow me." It is a command for us as well. We must go about our Father's business oblivious to the particular shape that other people's relationship with Jesus takes.

How Then Should We Act?

Immediately after my panic subsided at my friend's news, I began to think through how I should respond. I came up with the following nondefinitive list:

Take the long view. If I'm right that faith and unbelief in God are movements of the soul that take time before they manifest themselves externally, then I'm going to be patient and not try to immediately force him to see how he's wrong.

Take the God-centered view. This comes about through reading the Bible and praying. The more we recognize God's love for our friends, the more we'll be able to walk in that love with Him. And the more we realize that "all things are God's," including salvation, the less we will respond to decisions like my friend's with fear and anxiety. Instead we will be moved to prayer.

Take my friend's view. Because I was curious about why my friend left the faith, I proposed a future conversation about the reasons for his decision. I want to hear him out, and to answer his questions as well as I'm able. We'll talk apologetics, because we both enjoy a good debate. But for those who don't, I recommend addressing these topics with sensitivity.

Take my own view. In light of my friend's email, I have decided to do some good, solid self-examination. My fear that I said or did something that played a part in his leaving is real, and his decision gives me an opportunity to discern whether there are sins that I have committed for which I need to repent and ask forgiveness.

Take a joyful view. Drew Dyck, whose book *Generation Ex-Christian* addresses these issues in much more depth, offered this sage advice:

> I think too often when a friend or loved one strays from the faith we lose our joy. Our concern for their spiritual well-being actually causes us to adopt a dour demeanor and sabotages our witness. How do we expect them to want something that we don't appear to even enjoy?

There's a lot at stake in our friends' lives, but as Christians we need to constantly return to the source and center of our lives and to cultivate the sort of joy that exists in all circumstances.

BELONGING AFTER DISBELIEVING

When it comes to evangelism, the Christian community talks about "belonging before believing." We are to be hospitable and inviting. Before people enter a personal relationship with the triune God, we welcome them to come and see His redemptive power.

The same should be true of belonging after *disbelieving*. It's naïve to think that differences in belief won't alter the relationship. The grounds for our fellowship with other Christians are not our social connections or even the beliefs that we share, but rather the Spirit who is at work in our midst. Because those who reject Christianity reject these grounds for union, belonging after disbelieving in this sense is an impossibility.

But as Christians, we do have a fellowship with the world that can unite us. Inasmuch as they stand in need of redemption, so do we. It is a position that removes all grounds for boasting or judgment. When we recognize that, we can fellowship with them out of the love that Christ has for us.

And this is the opportunity before us: to love as Christ loves us and to give ourselves to others as He gave Himself for us. I don't know what will happen with my friend, or if he'll ever start attending church again. My calling is to love him regardless. And by God's mercy, I'll someday learn how to do just that.

A Confession of
Gratitude

───────── ❦ ─────────

No student, our Savior tells us, is greater than his teacher. That has never been more true here, which is why it is fitting to begin my confessions of gratitude by expanding on those to whom this book is dedicated: the faculty of the Torrey Honors Institute, and especially its founder, John Mark Reynolds, who is now Provost at Houston Baptist. John Mark's own deep love for goodness, truth, and beauty continue to challenge and inspire me—as does his willingness to enter into inquiry with those like me who are not his equals. The moment I met him I knew I was in crisis, that I had to either retreat or look along with him at the things he was striving to see. (This was not really a choice, though it seemed like one at the time.) Every Torrey student is his debtor, but me more than most. And if this book does not goad him to write better on this theme, then I have failed in my charge.

The other faculty were no less important to my experience at Torrey. They modeled integrating generous inquiry with a robust, full-throated affirmation of traditional Christianity. And their care and concern to understand the texts (even those we ended up disagreeing with!) never stood in the way of their deeper, more fundamental desire to encounter the truth and reality to which the texts could only point. How could I be the same after learning to love Calvin with the Wesleyan Fred Sanders, struggling through Locke with Paul Spears, rethinking *Orthodoxy* with Melissa Schubert, or reading Coleridge with Dan Yim?

Of course, it was my family who made that experience possible and who bore many of the growing pains as I struggled to learn that moderation and temperance apply to the intellectual life along with everything else. My parents, particularly, have been eager and encouraging supporters of this effort and had the foresight to care more deeply about my education well before I did. In virtue and character, in love and sacrifice, this son will not surpass his parents. And to my brother, particularly, thanks for the many epic conversations over the holidays where I learned the possibilities and limits of argument and what it takes to argue well. To the rest of my siblings, thanks for letting those happen, despite us not helping with the dishes. And to Jon, thanks for your inquiries, which have a way of going to the heart behind the matter.

There were many intellectual debts behind this book, some of which were stated in the text and others that lurk in the background. The most prominent is, of course, T. S. Eliot's magnificent *Four Quartets*. They are worth sitting with a good long while. I should highlight one other in particular: Paul Griffiths's *Intellectual Appetite* is a lovely book that gave me the courage, for good or ill, to explore the things themselves and write the words as I had them rather than repeatedly deferring to those who have said things better.

But many of my questions and ways of putting things were forged in practice, both in the classroom and beyond. I have mentioned the faculty of the Torrey Honors Institute: it would be wrong to not mention my peers, who sharpened and challenged me and often became friends. There are too many names to mention here, but to Olympia—thank you for being the greatest group ever in the history of Torrey so far. My Torrey Academy students were cheerful subjects of my dialectical experiments, and are sources of endless joy to me. This book is, I hope, some evidence of how much I learned from you all—though you probably did not realize it at the time. To Brian Nick, Rebecca Forte, and now Peter Gross of Wheatstone Academy, thank you for allowing me to partner with you through the years and encouraging me to share my thoughts with other tutors and teachers about how to help students question well.

I am blessed by the privilege of having friends whose grasp of these questions goes beyond my own and who were kind enough to provide feedback on this manuscript. Adam Green, particularly, engaged my work with the sort of care and attentiveness that a writer dreams about. Despite facing a move to Houston, Gary Hartenburg also provided very helpful comments, as did Isaac Wiegman, Jonathan Reibsamen, and Bob Hartman. Chloe Cuffel, Brian Trinh, Jeremy Mann, Jake Meador, Thomas Ward, and Fred Sanders were very gracious in extending timely words of challenge and feedback. Tyler Wigg-Stevenson, Brian Auten, Alastair Roberts, and Keith Buhler's incisive critiques improved the book in ways I hope they all recognize. And my debt to James Arnold extends beyond what words are able to capture. In the middle of a very busy time, he rescued *Mere Orthodoxy* from descending into total chaos, provided invaluable feedback on the manuscript, and stepped in to help with some laborious editorial work as well.

But I must make a special mention of Joe Carter, Daniel Suhr, and Andrew Walker, whose feedback on the manuscript was surpassed only by their patient and gracious friendship. Throughout the writing process, I repeatedly voiced frustrations and struggles with what I have taken as my vocation. Without them, I suspect I would have long ago given up the courage to continue on.

Similarly, Randall Payleitner and the team at Moody and my agent, Erik Wolgemuth, have been supportive and accepting of my idiosyncracies and neuroses. It is rare to find a publisher and agent so supportive of an author that they are willing to consider questioning the commonly received publishing wisdom about how to make books that find audiences. Randall and Erik have at each turn privileged the work itself, rather than sales, for which I cannot be more grateful. Brandon O'Brien provided incredibly helpful edits as well, without which this book would have been a good deal more cumbersome. Still, if I have failed in these pages to hit the mark, it is wholly my own fault.

A word about The Journey and Darrin Patrick: while many churches would have looked askance at me for my questioning, Darrin has gone the other direction and provided me the freedom and (occasionally!) the word of correction I have needed to not allow my intellectual life to be disconnected from my love for others. Darrin also once gave a sermon on questions and questioning that left me cheering. The rest of the staff and community at The Journey were similarly hospitable to me and have continued to be so.

All this and I have yet to mention Mere-O: as a community of readers and writers, I could not ask for a more successful experiment. Commenters are frequently derided by those who write online, but I am fortunate to be able to demur every single time. To those who have read and questioned, objected and explored, thank you. And to those writers who have chimed in, I have never been so happy to decrease as you all have increased. It is genuinely wonderful to be the least read and least popular writer there.

But there is one, one to whom I owe gratitude enough to fill every book I ever write: my wife, whose own explorations into God's inner life kept me praying through a season when I was sorely tempted to quit and whose ongoing care continues to be the most tangible expression of God's own love that I know. Words fail me here, which is probably best. You deserve gratitude in the form of my whole life, which is pledged to you in soul and body.

And what more shall I say? I do not have time to tell of all of Dustin Wilson's questions, of all I have learned from the "Sisters of Scottsdale," of Julie and her fearlessness in asking questions that others shrink from, of the new community of friends here in Oxford for whom these things are (thankfully!) nowhere near the "strictly academic," all those friends and fellow writers whose lives and inquiries have shaped my own, friends of whom the world simply is not worthy. To borrow a line from George Eliot, whatever good I have is due to the "unhistoric acts" of those who have "faithfully lived a hidden life." And they will be known by all when the Book of Life is finally read. *Sic transit gloria mundi*—the glory of the world fadeth away, but I will carry the glory and joy of their friendship and love deep in my heart until we all come together to the end of our exploring and our voices join in worship of the One whose love and friendship makes our own possible.

What's Next?

There is no real exploring except that which happens with others. You are already under way, if you have made it this far. It is probably best to speak with your pastor and ask for counsel and direction from this point forward. And if you are looking for a crash course in how to question well, you might contact the good folks at Wheatstone Ministries (wheatstoneministries.com). They've been doing this a long time and they are really good at what they do.

But you also might want to pick up another and (perhaps) a better book. Reading broadly and carefully helps us discover the strangeness of the world and the people in it. As we inhabit other people's perspectives by exploring the world along with them, we learn to ask their questions and so expand the range of questions we are able to explore.

What books should you turn to next? That's a good question. My provisional suggestion would be to turn back a generation, if you never have, and begin reading writers whose outlook and wordage is similar enough to our own that we can resonate with them, but also not so similar that they are one of us. C. S. Lewis is always a good read, particularly *Till We Have Faces,* and behind him G. K. Chesterton is worth exploring. T. S. Eliot's poetry is difficult, but rewarding. Austin Farrer, who I quoted several times, is an incredibly lucid writer who is both thoughtful and heartwarming. And those are merely a beginning: They are each, in their own way, gateways to a world of more riches and depths.

As for me, with all God's grace I shall continue my explorations. If you wish to join me or contact me for any reason, email me at matthewleeanderson.84@gmail.com. I'm also on Facebook, if it is still a thing when you read this, at facebook.com/matthewleeanderson. And for the lovers of short-form thoughts, you may chase me at Twitter at @mattleeanderson.

I may answer your questions with questions, because I can. Consider yourself forewarned.

And we shall keep on at Mere Orthodoxy, the place online that comes closest to home for me. We may converse there and explore some of the avenues and angles that went unexplored in these pages. Or we may turn in new directions, as we see fit. But as God is merciful, with each step we will move strive to move closer toward the one who in whom all our desires will finally come to rest, the one who has already made possible our rest for us.

moody
collective

Moody Collective brings words of life to a generation seeking deeper faith. We are a part of Moody Publishers, representing this next generation of followers of Christ through books, blogs, essays, and more.

We seek to know, love, and serve the millennial generation with grace and humility. Each of our books is intended to challenge and encourage our readers as they pursue God. To learn more, visit our website, www.moodycollective.com.

MOODY
PUBLISHERS

www.MoodyPublishers.com